2287

KATRINA

Mississippi Women Remember

Mississippi State Committee of the National Museum of Women in the Arts

Photography by Melody Golding   Edited by Sally Pfister

University Press of Mississippi   *Jackson*

www.upress.state.ms.us

The University Press of Mississippi is a member of the Association
    of American University Presses.

Compilation copyright © 2007 by the Mississippi State Committee
    of the National Museum of Women in the Arts

Manufactured in Canada

First edition 2007

Library of Congress Cataloging-in-Publication Data

Katrina : Mississippi women remember / edited by Sally Pfister ; photography by Melody Golding. — 1st ed.

    p. cm.

    ISBN-13: 978-1-57806-956-9 (cloth : alk. paper)

    ISBN-10: 1-57806-956-4 (cloth : alk. paper)   1.   Gulf Coast
(Miss.)—History—21st century—Anecdotes. 2.   Hurricane Katrina,
2005—Anecdotes. 3.   Women—Mississippi—Gulf Coast—Biography—Anecdotes. 4.   Disaster victims—Gulf Coast—Biography—Anecdotes. 5.   Gulf Coast (Miss.)—Biography—Anecdotes. 6.   Gulf
Coast (Miss.)—Social conditions—21st century—Anecdotes. 7. Hurricane Katrina, 2005—Pictorial works. 8. Gulf Coast (Miss.)—Social
conditions—21st century—Pictorial works. I. Pfister, Sally. II. Golding, Melody. III. National Museum of Women in the Arts (U.S.). Mississippi State Committee.

    F347.G9K38 2007

    976'.044—dc22   2006100155

British Library Cataloging-in-Publication Data available

This project is dedicated to the thousands of men and women on the Mississippi Gulf Coast who were so devastatingly affected by this catastrophic storm, and to the gracious women who so generously shared their amazing stories with us all.

To my husband Steve, without whose unselfish support and encouragement it would not ever have become a reality, and to my sons whose continued love and belief propelled me forward.

I thank God for the ability, faith, and vision for this project.

—MELODY GOLDING

I dedicate this book with grateful affection to Gladys Kemp Lisanby, chair of the Katrina Project. If not for her guidance and support it would never have come together.

—SALLY PFISTER

Foreword

On the morning of August 29, 2005, Hurricane Katrina, ravaged the Mississippi Gulf Coast with winds approaching 140 m.p.h. and a tidal surge exceeding twenty-four feet.

From the Alabama line to the Louisiana delta and for a hundred miles inland, the scene by that afternoon was one of complete devastation. Homes were flattened and splintered, public buildings destroyed, and the fabric of Gulf Coast living, as generations had known it, was torn asunder. The damage extended far inland, with widespread power outages, torrential rains, and high winds.

The impact on the personal lives of tens of thousands of coastal residents was no less traumatic than the twisted landscape. Beyond the more than one thousand lives lost to the storm, individual lives had been changed forever.

In the weeks to follow, as trucks and bulldozers worked to even the landscape, the glow of an inner spark was soon in evidence among those who stayed and labored amidst the debris and ruin. From somewhere deep within the human spirit the will to live and to rebuild broken lives proved to be unquenchable.

Among the first to share in this rebirth have been our Mississippi women artists, with their strength, empathy, and vision of a better future for Mississippi, their communities, and their art.

Told through the bold, stark reality of the camera lens of Mississippi artist Melody Golding and in the words of the individuals who lived through those tragic early days, this is perhaps the best and truest test of the human spirit: to have what it takes to absorb the hardest blows of life and respond in beauty and with a love of life that transcends tragedy, that turns defeat into praise and desolation into hope.

Melody Golding records these images with the expectation that they will survive this day, even as the spirit of the individual artists will survive these troubled times. We hope that this record of a difficult time in the history of our beloved state will serve a higher purpose to mold and shape the future of each of us, as well as those who follow along in years to come.

There is nothing so strong and powerful that it cannot be made better through the eye of the artist.

—Gladys Kemp Lisanby
Founding President
The Mississippi State Committee
National Museum of Women in the Arts

Preface

This book of photographs by Melody Golding and words by Mississippi women about Hurricane Katrina documents the devastation of the Mississippi Gulf Coast and the resilience and determination of the people of Mississippi most deeply affected by that catastrophic storm. Our goal in writing it is to provide a lasting testament to the events that Katrina set in motion. As time inevitably moves on, it seems entirely fitting and appropriate to reflect on the experiences and challenges of those whose lives were changed forever on August 29, 2005. This book provides a unique and very personal perspective.

In the early days following Katrina, Melody Swaney Golding, a noted photographer from Vicksburg, came to the coast as a Red Cross volunteer, bringing supplies and a desire to help. Her photographic journal and memories of those days are stunning in their powerful simplicity. Early on, Melody believed these photographs could serve as the basis of a book of significant interest.

At the same time, the Mississippi State Committee of the National Museum of Women in the Arts, of which Melody is a member, was also on a mission. This group, which encourages the work of women artists in Mississippi, is part of a network that advances the mission of NMWA in Washington, D.C., the only major museum in the world devoted to women artists.

Two weeks after Katrina, this message went out via e-mail to the closely knit group:

Since last we were in touch, Hurricane Katrina has come and gone and changed our lives in so many ways. Many of our members have lost their homes and their belongings and are now helping friends and family start anew.

The impact this storm has had on all of us is stunning and far-reaching, and the ripple effect goes on and on. Many of you have been in touch as best you can and we hope you will continue to check in and let us know how you are doing.

There is a spray-painted sign on battered Beach Boulevard in Pascagoula that says "Don't let Katrina steal your joy." To that we add Amen.

The response to that message and succeeding messages spoke to the concern and caring that members of the group showed for one another. It was remarkable that so many took the time to reach out, considering the widespread displacement and upheaval of the time.

In October 2005, Melody Golding contacted the Mississippi State Committee founder and president, Gladys Kemp Lisanby, to offer her photographs for a different kind of book about Katrina. As a seventh-generation Mississippian, Melody knew the indomitable strength, spirit, and courage of the people of her state. We called on members of the Mississippi State Committee, and asked for their Katrina experiences. For many, writing these stories was an almost impossible task. It was all too painful, too wrenching, too raw in those early days.

As the first grim days passed and the initial shock lessened, the harsh new realities of life set in. What to do? Where to start? Where and how will we live in the midst of all this chaos and destruction? Shall we rebuild? Can we rebuild? Who will help us?

The decisive leadership of Governor Haley Barbour set the tone. By quickly convening a task force to address the many complex issues involved in rebuilding the Gulf Coast, he provided the right approach and attitude. There was a tremendous response from everyday people everywhere, as they put their own lives on hold to come and offer their help. Churches and faith-based groups from many states came and worked and stayed, and they remain in many communities where the needs are never ending. We are humbled by their generosity and selflessness. Countless meals were provided by such familiar disaster-relief agencies as the Salvation Army and the American Red Cross, and the National Guardsmen were our heroes.

There were endless lines for everything, with food and gas in short supply and available housing next to impossible to find. The relentless heat and humidity made it that much harder to cope. Gradually, temporary housing began appearing, government issued and otherwise. The massive debris piles slowly began shrinking. There were small satisfactions as people found bits and pieces of their belongings, sometimes unbelievably far afield. A point of deposit was established in many neighborhoods where people could drop off found items and, it was hoped, retrieve some of their own. These also served as a central spot for meeting and exchanging information. Not only did you now know all of your neighbors' names, you also knew what their needs were.

The insurance companies were overwhelmed, as were their frantic clients, and satisfactory solutions were hard to come by. To the insurers, a chair was a chair and a painting a painting, not a treasured family heirloom. So many lost so much, and there were no easy answers. Contractors and roofers came and went, with some providing hope and others spreading further despair. New government guidelines on rebuilding were slow in coming and in many cases created more problems than they solved. Depression and apathy were the order of the day, and many sank into a limbo of waiting and ennui.

But it is not in our nature to exist this way for long, and as time passed the somber mood gradually began to lift. "Stuff," as everyone called it, didn't matter so much any more. Old friendships remained strong, for all that they were now long-distance in nature, and significant new relationships formed. Although this ordeal is by no means over and will not be over for a very long time, there are hopeful signs of new growth and rebuilding.

The members of the Mississippi State Committee have opened their hearts to join their stories and remembrances with Melody's photographs to tell the story they lived. They paint a mesmerizing picture of this unforgettable chapter in Mississippi history.

—Sally Pfister

Photographer's Preface

When Hurricane Katrina came ashore on August 29, 2005, there was no question that she would be powerful and destructive. By all accounts from national weather forecasting and predictions, this was "the big one."

Katrina hit land with sustained winds of 140 miles per hour and a storm surge 200 miles wide and 25 to 30 feet high. A Category 4 storm, she was officially less powerful than the legendary Camille, a 1969 Category 5 that has served as the standard for many years. But Katrina was much larger and meaner. With her much more destructive storm surge and with hurricane-force winds extending out 120 miles from the center, Katrina swept across three states and 250 miles of coastline.

More than a thousand people died. Three large cities, including New Orleans, and countless small towns and communities were wrecked. More than half a million homes and businesses were destroyed and 1.4 million people were displaced. Officially it is the single worst natural disaster to have ever occurred on U.S. soil in our recorded history.

There was no way that the people throughout Mississippi and Louisiana could have prepared for the destruction and devastation that occurred that day. Those of us who were relatively out of harm's way felt the urgency of the outer bands of Katrina, and we were glued to our TVs and radios as the storm skipped Florida and neared land, putting the

Mississippi Gulf Coast in the northeast quadrant of the storm, where the storm is most powerful. We could see it was only a matter of time before it was too late for those who had decided to remain behind and ride out the storm.

A number of evacuees fled to our home, in Vicksburg, from the path of the storm. My husband Steve strongly encouraged them to come as quickly as possible when they called, as Katrina was growing larger by the hour out in the Gulf. Some had driven for as many as twelve to thirteen hours in endless traffic on Mississippi highways, a journey that normally takes two or three hours. We were thankful that they had come to stay with us and that they sought and found safe shelter away from the eye of where the storm was predicted to land.

One of our evacuees was my husband's sister Carol Ann from Ocean Springs, Mississippi. Frank, her husband, made the decision to ride out the storm there, and we didn't know for several days whether or not he had survived. When we finally heard from him, we learned he was miraculously unharmed and their home had sustained only a little damage.

Telephones and cell phones worked erratically or not at all, and communication was virtually nonexistent. People were frantic about their families, their loved ones, their neighbors and friends.

We were so worried for our son Austin who is a student at Mississippi State University where they had high winds and threatening weather from the outer bands of Katrina. Many parents of the students at Mississippi State, who are from the coast, even sought refuge with their children and stayed with them there in the dorms. The university welcomed them.

Our son John Reid who is in high school here in Vicksburg found a local church shelter, immediately after the storm, that had opened its doors for refugees, and he was helping with finding desperately needed items. He gathered blankets and pillows and bedding for those who went to the shelters and had nowhere else to go. His actions were such an inspiration to me. There was no rest, in our own home, in knowing that so many were suffering so greatly.

It was when I had offered to drive Carol Ann back home to Ocean Springs that I decided also to take supplies in my car from the American Red Cross. This would be my first trip to the Mississippi Gulf Coast since Katrina hit, just eight days after.

At the Red Cross Shelter in Vicksburg, they packed gallons and gallons of water, about six hundred meals ready to eat (MREs), first-aid items, CARE packages, cases of other various canned food items, and baby supplies into my Suburban. My instructions were to give the items to "whoever needed it." They said that I would know who needed help when I saw them.

My car was so heavy that I had to put extra air in the tires, and then I had to wait in long lines for hours for gasoline. Everyone across the south was experiencing the crunch of the gas shortage because of the hurricane. People were in a panic at the possibility of no fuel to be had. I brought along an extra five-gallon container of gas because rumor had it that there was none to be had south of Hattiesburg.

In a small corner of my vehicle, I stashed my camera bag, cameras, and a lot of film. I knew that this horrific event must be recorded, and although I am an artist/photographer and not a photojournalist, I was determined to document to the best of my ability, as a native Mississippian, the travesty that had happened in our beloved state. There was no way that I could just sit back and do nothing.

As I drove down Highway 49, we started seeing destruction in Hattiesburg, about eighty miles north of Gulfport. There were downed trees and power lines, and the highway was littered with debris. As we drove further south, the debris piles grew. From Interstate 10 south, trees were barren and bent at an inward angle, as if a giant hand had shoved them aside and stripped them of all foliage. The stately and famous live oaks, now sadly leaning, were devoid of leaves and covered in a putrid mud, with all manner of things hanging from their limbs.

It was incredible to know that this vast destruction had come from just a few hours of the pounding of a Category 4 hurricane. Though it was barely September, it had the look of a desolate winter landscape, and everywhere you looked you saw a very surrealistic scene. It reminded me of the photographs we have all seen of bombed-out cities in war-ravaged Europe and Japan from World War II. It honestly looked as if a nuclear bomb had gone off, and for as far as the eye could see.

We made it into Ocean Springs, picked up Carol Ann's husband Frank at their home, and then drove carefully and slowly around downed and broken trees and power lines and debris on to the beach road. Nothing could have prepared us for what we saw there. As far as we could see there was virtually nothing left of the once-charming and beautiful coastline. Our hearts broke as we saw that in town after town, from Pascagoula westward to Waveland and Bay St. Louis, the destruction and devastation was nearly complete. The tragic loss of life and the incredible decimation of the very fabric of the lives of fellow human beings was too much to bear.

As I maneuvered along the coastline, I had to drive back out to I-10 to get from town to town because the bridges had been mangled and destroyed like a child's stack of toys. There were giant piles of rubble and cracked wood and sodden pieces of broken furniture scattered in the streets. What was once the very essence of people's lives now had been reduced to piles of rotting and foul-smelling splinters of wood and trash.

In some places the sea had simply washed clean the landscape and taken what was in its path entirely back out to the sea. In other places there was the sickly sweet and cloying smell of death and decay.

Now sacred ground, where once children played and birds sang and people thrived, a deafening silence and only the traces of the lost communities lingered. The very air was lifeless and held me in the grip of a smothering and dying atmosphere. The only things left behind seemed to be the plastic and paper which hung everywhere in the leafless trees, sometimes flapping in the wind. Ripped bed sheets and clothing and carpets were wrapped around fallen fences and branches, trees, anywhere that it may have suddenly stopped from the surge of the sea, and it was evident that an incredible struggle had ensued.

Most of the debris was undistinguishable, but here and there were items that had once been a part of a life: a broken tea cup, a baby's shoe, an old record, a child's twisted tricycle, a sodden and once-beloved toy stuffed animal, a bottle of bug spray, and multicolored Mardi Gras beads which had been flung high into the trees by gale force winds. Here and there would be a broken piece of someone's prized porcelain collection, a treasured family photograph now torn and covered in mold, a broken and twisted hard-earned trophy, a pair of silk panties hanging from a tree branch . . .

American flags respectfully flew everywhere. In many cases, they were draped across steps—for many the only thing left of their homes. The flags honored the very ground where thriving Americans had been the week before, complete lives full of hope and promise. Now all that remained was their injured pride, and they were showing it through the display of our national symbol, the flag.

The sons and daughters of the military were out in force, the Navy, the Army, the Air Force, and the Marines. The National Guard and also the Coast Guard—they were all there, and in their strength and training came to the rescue of their fellow Americans, many of whom had been knocked to their knees and left breathless and heaving, stripped of all but the very clothes on their backs. We offered these soldiers bottled water as we drove along in the sweltering ninety-degree-plus heat, but invariably they said, "No thank you, give the water to someone else who needs it." They all are to be commended for a job well done and bravely carried out.

On I drove across the destroyed Mississippi Gulf Coast as Carol Ann softly cried in the back seat of my car, and Frank told me where we were. All landmarks were gone and we could only guess at our exact location. We gave the bottled water and food, the bare essentials for living, to people who were now living sparingly on the beach in tattered tents. As I navigated down the narrow alleyways that had once been beautiful tree-lined streets of charming coastal neighborhoods, I passed piles of rubble higher than the roof of my car. Seeing the haunted looks of utter disbelief in the eyes of the victims is unforgettable and excruciating to have witnessed. These folks all had a story of their own personal survival to tell. Whether their homes were flooded by just a few inches of water and were now covered in decaying black mold, or whether the homes were entirely washed away, they were all sadly in a state of utter shock, disbelief, and pathos.

Amid the chaos in the aftermath of the storm, other than the troops, we saw very few people on that first trip. Most people had evacuated before the storm and had not yet returned. Rescue teams from all around the country were valiantly working to restore order, remove bodies, aid the living, and curb any lawlessness or looting. Large bulldozers were clearing the broken and twisted Highway 90, which in some areas had completely disappeared, and in others had been picked up and moved inland by the awesome strength of the surging waters.

When I returned to the Gulf Coast, several weeks later, to meet with the amazing people who were bravely piecing back together their lives, and to try to photograph history in the making, I saw the humanitarian tent cities which churches across our nation had set up to assist in the recovery. Composed of all denominations, these makeshift communities offered hot meals, beds, and showers to the newly homeless population.

FEMA, the Federal Emergency Management Agency, had begun bringing in the 22 x 9 foot trailers for those many people who were living in small tents and sleeping on the cold and unforgiving ground of school ball fields. They had nowhere else to go. All hotel rooms were full of evacuees as far north as Memphis, Tennessee, as far west as Texas, and as far east as Florida. It was so hard to believe that all of this was happening in our America.

These people all along the Mississippi Gulf Coast were stripped of the very makeup of what defines a life, in terms of their material belongings. However, they have proved that what truly defines a person is not in the possessions that they own but who they are in their hearts and souls. Bravely and resolutely the Gulf Coast will be rebuilt by these amazing Americans, and their strength and determination will be an inspiration to us all, through these very painful times of adversity and strife.

Traveling to and from the coast, month after month with my cameras within the year following Katrina, state line to state line, community after community, I have come to know so many wonderful and amazing people—people from all walks of life and representing all sectors of society, who have shared their stories and lives with me, not just of heartbreak but of inspiration and hope, and for that I will be forever grateful.

It will be years, possibly even a generation, before the Mississippi Gulf Coast shows a significant recovery from the wrath and destruction of the infamous Hurricane Katrina. But the Gulf Coast is slowly beginning the process of rebuilding now, and even though it will never be exactly the same as before, perhaps in some ways it will be an even better place in the future. Somewhere, in the sand and the rubble, the charm and the soul of a region are still there.

The resilience of the human spirit was the one thing that Katrina simply could not wash away.

These photographs are the result of my year-long journeys to the Mississippi Gulf Coast, starting shortly after Hurricane Katrina came ashore through August 2006, from Pearlington to Pascagoula, state line to state line. They are my personal witness to the events of this sweeping and nondiscriminating catastrophe. I am honored to have been a part of documenting this epic storm and to have shared in my telling of it through the gifts which God has given me in my photography.

It is an incomplete visual recording of the Mississippi Gulf coastline, which very nearly had life and hope wrung out of it after the storm. These images radically simplify what really happened. My goal in capturing them was to convey the essence of the hurricane's destruction. The grim subject matter has a nightmarish quality, yet also a strangely elegant observance as we attempt to visualize the experiences of the victims of the storm.

The words that accompany the photographs are from the extraordinary people of Mississippi who experienced profound loss due to the storm. They are personal and heartbreaking, yet some are incredibly uplifting with messages of hope. Hurricane Katrina is a painful reminder that nature does not always have mercy, no matter our circumstances or station in life, and that any one of us may be tested terribly at any moment by the times in which we live.

What a paradox, in which the women of Mississippi find themselves once again tested in the crucible of history. Like the remarkable females of the South in generations past who have been tried over and over again in piecing their lives back together after the devastation of civil war, crippling depression, cruel social injustices, and previous natural disasters, they let us see that a familiar chord runs unchained in the hearts and souls of these determined, proud, genteel, and strong women of the twenty-first century once again. Their suffering, and the dignified ways in which they deal with it historically, have ennobled women in the South. How they overcome the adversities they have faced is an inspiration to all. They are truly "steel magnolias."

This book is a very personal journal and will provide historical testimony, both literally and visually, for future generations. Mississippians comprise this book completely. Its very identity arises from the photographs and the stories by women within this state.

Katrina: Mississippi Women Remember provides an important and unique record, and I hope that people will return to its pages again and again to ponder the sheer enormity of this epic storm from such a personal viewpoint. The idyllic life we once knew on the Mississippi Gulf Coast is for now only a dream from the past. However, it will again rise from the rubble and one day become the elegant and charming southern lady she once was.

—Melody Golding

Acknowledgments

We thank the people of Mississippi who have so generously contributed their Hurricane Katrina experiences. Their stories must never be forgotten.

Special thanks to
Dr. Judy L. Larson, Director; Dr. Susan Fisher Sterling, Deputy Director and Senior Curator; Ilene Gutman, Director of National and International Affairs; and Elizabeth S. G. Nicholson, Editor-in-Chief, the National Museum of Women in the Arts

Dr. Patricia L. Pinson, Curator, the Walter Anderson Museum of Art

Lucy Allen, Museum Division Director, Mississippi Department of Archives and History

Anita Giani, editorial support

Frank and Carol Ann Wilkerson, for their invaluable assistance on locations and landmarks

Gwen Impson

Contributors

Ann Arledge, Joan G. Armstrong, Lyn Bailey, Maria Baisier, Cookie Bello, Missy Bennett, Ann Lisanby Bianchi, Kathy Blazer, Betty Slay Bradley, Lyn Shoemaker Brown, Marjorie Butterworth, Kristin Byrd, Claudia Cartee, Marti Anderson Cockrell, Kristian Dambrino, Mary Ott Davidson, Betty Dettre, Penny Sanford Fikes, Lou Fontaine, Ellen Gilchrist, Melody Golding, Marjie Gowdy, Ann Guice, Nancy Guice, Joey Hammock Halinski, Lisa Hammack, Mary Hardy, Gwen Impson, Martha Dunn Kirkley, Jean Laney, Gladys Kemp Lisanby, Sarah H. Lisanby, M.D., Katherine Lochridge, Mendy Mayfield, Dena McKee, Melanie Reimer Moore, Susie W. Moran, Martha Moss, Patt Odom, Betty Oswald, Thaou Thi (Kim) Pham, Mary Anderson Pickard, Patricia Pinson, Elizabeth D. Schafer, Dell Dickins Scoper, Michelle Drane Smith, Opal Smith, Nancy Spiker, Christa Stapp, Lois Swaney, Ruth Thompson, Stacy Waites, Germaine Weldon

KATRINA

September 2005, Pascagoula

again in piecing their lives back together after the devastation of civil war, crippling depression, cruel social injustices, and previous natural disasters, they let us see that a familiar chord runs unchained in the hearts and souls of these determined, proud, genteel, and strong women of the twenty-first century once again. Their suffering, and the dignified ways in which they deal with it historically, have ennobled women in the South. How they overcome the adversities they have faced is an inspiration to all. They are truly "steel magnolias."

This book is a very personal journal and will provide historical testimony, both literally and visually, for future generations. Mississippians comprise this book completely. Its very identity arises from the photographs and the stories by women within this state.

Katrina: Mississippi Women Remember provides an important and unique record, and I hope that people will return to its pages again and again to ponder the sheer enormity of this epic storm from such a personal viewpoint. The idyllic life we once knew on the Mississippi Gulf Coast is for now only a dream from the past. However, it will again rise from the rubble and one day become the elegant and charming southern lady she once was.

—Melody Golding

Acknowledgments

We thank the people of Mississippi who have so generously contributed their Hurricane Katrina experiences. Their stories must never be forgotten.

Special thanks to

Dr. Judy L. Larson, Director; Dr. Susan Fisher Sterling, Deputy Director and Senior Curator; Ilene Gutman, Director of National and International Affairs; and Elizabeth S. G. Nicholson, Editor-in-Chief, the National Museum of Women in the Arts

Dr. Patricia L. Pinson, Curator, the Walter Anderson Museum of Art

Lucy Allen, Museum Division Director, Mississippi Department of Archives and History

Anita Giani, editorial support

Frank and Carol Ann Wilkerson, for their invaluable assistance on locations and landmarks

Gwen Impson

September 2005, Biloxi
Historic Beauvoir: A competitive spirit
against the ravages of the storm

September 2005

September 2005, Ocean Springs
Military on patrol to prevent looting
shortly after the storm

September 2005, Ocean Springs

Bridge to Biloxi from Ocean Springs,
Hwy. 90

September 2005, Gulfport

September 2005, Biloxi

Treasure Bay Casino (later demolished)

September 2005, Gulfport
Grand Casino that washed across Hwy.
90 in tidal surge (demolished)

September 2005, Pass Christian
Cleanup crew in parking lot

September 2005, Gulfport

FEMA workers and steps to nowhere . . .

September 2005, Gulfport

City street

September 2005, Biloxi
Military serviceman, tired and hot

September 2005, Biloxi

Slant House

September 2005, Ocean Springs

Weldon home site

September 2005

September 2005, Biloxi
Servicemen resting from a full day
of work

September 2005

U.S. Hwy. 90

September 2005, Ocean Springs
Shearwater Bridge, Carol Ann Wilkerson

September 2005, Ocean Springs

Sailboats displaced after tidal surge

September 2005, Ocean Springs

Ocean Springs Harbor—boats on land,
not water

September 2005, Biloxi
Remains of "Shark Head" gift shop
and office complex

KATRINA

AN INTRODUCTION

ELLEN GILCHRIST   Ocean Springs

I am fiercely and horribly proud to be a Mississippian. Never more so than when I read the essays by these women. Our pioneer ancestors came to this state in many ways, some in chains and some on flatboats down the Ohio and Mississippi Rivers, some carrying flat silver and bibles and rolls of fabric and heads full of dreams and engineering skills, a few were doctors and many of the women knew how to care for the sick and wounded. They brought dogs bred in England and Scotland and Wales, rat terriers and retrievers and pointers for hunting birds and deer and squirrels. They made friends with the Chickasaw Indians and sometimes married them and learned their ways.

They brought to the untamed state of Mississippi the fabulous heritage of Western Civilization and built brick churches and frame churches out of bricks they made and wood they planed. They had skills and tools and they cleared the land and began to build.

They left behind these daughters, proud, brave, resourceful, unsentimental women who are as much pioneers as their ancestors.

These women took all that Katrina could hand out and fought back as brave women have always done. They took care of the weak and sick and dying, they ran to higher ground and they started to rebuild. Living in tents and trailers they hooked up their computers to batteries and made a record of what they had endured and how they are beginning to repair the damage, not only to the physical structures that were destroyed and flooded but to the hearts and minds and souls of their families and each other.

The schools of Mississippi were started by men and women who read Shakespeare and the Greek and Roman philosophers and believed in poetry and literature and the rule of law. Even our worst schools, in our smallest hamlets, in our darkest, poorest times, have taught literature. Our children were taught poems and limericks and songs and read to out of the great literature of the British Isles. They were raised on tales of bravery, moral fables, stories that taught them to be wary of cunning foxes and alligators offering rides across rivers. This literature taught cunning and self-reliance and fortitude, "the strength to bear misfortune and pain calmly and patiently, firm courage." The kind of courage that allows one to face a calamity with grit, backbone, guts, pluck. True Grit was what we admired in John Wayne. Our literary heroines were plucky girls. You could not starve them into submission. They fought back and they survived and triumphed.

These tales resonated in the minds of many when the bad August storm came and blew away so much of what we had built and created.

When I called Ocean Springs after the storm the first thing people told me was that the High School and the library and the Walter Anderson museum had survived. Many of the essays in this book are by women from Ocean Springs and its sister communities, Biloxi, Gulfport, Gautier, Bay Saint Louis, Pass Christian, Diamondhead, Pearlington, Pascagoula, Holly Springs, Moss Point, Kilmichael. Just to write the names of the towns is to hear Mississippians' love for words.

I have a condominium on the beach in Ocean Springs. We are rebuilding these apartments and I had a letter the other day from the board of directors saying we are now going to call them townhouses. I giggled for an hour after I read the letter. That is so Mississippian that I don't know how to explain the humor of it to anyone from another state.

The woman who washed off the CD needed to reprogram her computer in her newly installed replacement toilet (which was the only source of water in the house) is the sort of woman I want with me when disaster strikes. Her brilliant, elegant essay is on page 65. She is from Gautier, a small town near Ocean Springs. Especially beautiful girls from Gautier took dance classes with my granddaughters. The reason I have a townhouse (nee, condominium) on the beach in Ocean Springs was so I would be there to drive my granddaughters to dance classes at Donna's School of Visual and Performing Arts, as their mother was busy working for a living in the afternoons. Another highlight of early talks with Ocean Springs residents was reports that Donna's dance floors had been flooded. The Yoga school across the street, however, was reported to have survived, as had the new South American dressmaker who had set up shop on Washington Avenue.

It is important to understand the significance people in Mississippi give to art and beauty, to education and dance and painting and literature and the rule of law in order to understand how they have begun to rebuild the coast so quickly while other places are still struggling to begin.

Mississippi women can't stand to look at a mess. It's hardwired in our genes. We have to make things beautiful. We have to teach young girls to dance and praise painters and put up with writers while they are learning their trade.

We also love and honor engineers and physicians and scientists. As housewives we love carpenters and electricians and plumbers and roofers and yard men. You can't create beauty unless you get the men to do the heavy lifting.

"He huffed and he puffed and he blew the house down" is a line that kept resonating in my mind as I walked along the beaches of Ocean Springs and Gulfport and Biloxi after the storm and remembered the beautiful beach houses where I had visited all my life. The casinos where I had never spent more than twenty dollars in quarters on any day except for one night when I lost sixty dollars by making the mistake of moving to the dollar slots. Beauvoir, the home of Jefferson Davis, where my grandmother visited as a child and later copied the treehouse in the front yard when she had been transported by marriage to a small town in Alabama. The treehouse had broad white stairs and wrapped around an oak tree like a veranda (Mississippian for porch). My grandmother and her friends would have tea in the treehouse on nice days. When one of their group became too crippled to climb the stairs they had tea on the porch of the house instead and looked at the treehouse. No lady from Mississippi would climb a set of stairs in front of someone too crippled to accompany them.

It is difficult to explain to someone from a less polite culture how much these things mattered when a storm came and blew away the homes and livelihoods of thousands of our citizens. Many homeless people lived with relatives in other towns, many were bivouacked in Jackson, which had little electricity, phone service, or gasoline for several weeks.

People did not complain or wait for the government to come save them. They saved each other and they saved themselves. The government was generous and so were thousands of out-of-state people who came to help clean up the mess and the people of Mississippi are grateful for that help but they didn't wait on it or depend on it. As these essays attest they went to work as soon as their feet were dry to clean up the mess and rebuild their towns.

Another important thing is how easily they gave up the STUFF that had been washed out to sea. The Gulf of Mexico off the coast of Mississippi is called the Mississippi Sound. Currently it is awash in silver, china, pottery, paintings, photographs—baby pictures, wedding albums, photographs of soldiers, sailors, and Marines, prom photographs, beauty contest and dance recital photographs, graduation photographs, photographs of young men on football and basketball and soccer and tennis and golf teams, girls in homecoming dresses and young men in tuxedos. To count the losses is useless. It is all out there in the water. A wave of water came in and sucked everything back out into the sea. Antique furniture made in Mississippi by Mississippi hands from Mississippi cypress and pine and cedar and walnut and cherry trees, beautiful pleated draperies and lace curtains and plantation blinds (horribly expensive, I never could bring myself to buy any, but my mother did), pots and pans and towels and sheets and pillows and pillowcases and hand-knitted afghans and embroidered alphabets, framed and saved by the mothers of the girls who embroidered them. Saved for posterity. Well, posterity is here and we have to press on with the alphabet in our heads. It turns out floods can't suck memories out into the sea unless they kill us to do it.

Anyway, all that STUFF washed out to sea and the women who had been in charge of it have achieved a fatalistic attitude about that STUFF that amazes me when they talk or write about it. These women know the real stuff of life was not in those lost rooms. The true grit and guts and pluck and purpose is to press on and save the babies. A woman in one of these essays put a baby in a piece of Tupperware to transfer it from a small sinking boat to a larger rescue vehicle. I adore the image of that fat, handsome baby riding the waves in a piece of Tupperware. Tupperware is so strong, designed to survive years of use in real kitchens. I never doubted for a second that the baby was safe.

There is a mystical, biblical feel to these essays. These women, and so many like them in this land of history and fiction, poetry and plays, actors and actresses both on and off the stage, gardeners, decorators, and homemakers par excellence, reflect this mystical love of beauty and order in their essays. Hooray for them for making this record of their travails and adventures.

It would be good if I stopped writing now and let their accounts speak for themselves.

HOW DO YOU KNOW?

LYN SHOEMAKER BROWN   Gautier

We had lived on Beach Boulevard in Pascagoula for thirty-seven years in a home we designed with an architect. We loved living on the beach because of the view and the breezes . . . we could look out and see all the way to the islands ten miles south of us. Our three children loved sailing, fishing, and all the other things kids do.

They grew up, went to college, and all found new lives as college graduates. Raymond and I were still there, growing older and dealing with what seemed like more and more hurricanes every year.

I became worried as the years passed that there would be a big storm which would wipe us out. I guess older people tend to worry more than the young. With storms on my mind much of the time, one night I dreamed I was flying over my house after there had been a big storm which had washed away all the homes, and I turned to someone flying next to me and said, "That is where my home was," and pointed to a slab below.

The person said, "How do you know?"

I said, "I can see my beautiful tile floors."

After I finally convinced my husband that we needed to sell our home while it was still intact, we sold it and moved to a new home we built in the woods of Gautier. We call it our tree house, because we live on the second level, where we can easily see birds.

And a little over a year later, on the second day after Hurricane Katrina, our son, who lives in Houston, flew over the Pascagoula-Gautier area, checking on our new house in the woods and also flying over our former home where he had grown up.

Days later when phone service was restored, the conversation with my son was almost like the one in my dream.

The house we lived in for thirty-seven years was gone, leaving a slab with colorful tile floors.

DEBRIS AND MORE

JOAN G. ARMSTRONG   Ocean Springs

The grim weather report very early Sunday morning that stated Category 5 Katrina would be at my door in less than twenty-four hours left me unable to move for a while. It was terrible news, as my condo is at twenty feet of elevation, right on the Gulf of Mexico. I had lugged so many things upstairs in preparation for last year's Ivan, but this time I didn't think it would help.

Frantic calls started coming in from my children, and I ended up evacuating to daughter Jill's house in Mexico Beach, Florida. A friend drove me, a dog, and a cat, and we ended up with nine other people in a two-bedroom house. All the facilities worked, but space was definitely limited. Jill told me that when she saw the Weather Channel's Jim Cantore in Biloxi, she yelled to the TV for him to go home and get out of her mama's backyard!

We were able to see the debris line on the computer but unable to communicate with friends and relatives who we knew had stayed behind. It was an extremely anxious time. My son Terry is in the National Guard in Iraq and actually got his two weeks' leave while we were evacuated to Florida. This was a blessing on so many levels, as we really needed him. When we were able to return to the beachfront in Ocean

Springs, I realized that I had made a serious mistake in not moving my belongings upstairs: this time the upstairs did stay dry, but the downstairs was a complete loss. Terry got to work cutting down trees, going through the debris piles, and packing me out of what was left of my home until it was time for him to get back on the plane. He just went from one war zone to another and back again. My disadvantaged son was so very willing to help if he was able, and my other children, a son and two daughters from near and far, all assembled to help and reunite with Terry. It was a great joy to me.

The debris piles were mesmerizing. It was hard to stay away from them, to not keep digging through them. I lost some of my paintings and actually found one or two in the debris pile, though not the ones I had recently been working on. I was having trouble with the spiral in my current piece, and Katrina finished it for me and kept the painting. A sculpture that I consider my most prized possession was in my washed-through downstairs, and I thought it was gone forever. Somehow it survived unharmed, and through the kindness of friends was kept safe and sound for my return.

Some neighbors who had a wonderful older Greek Revival home next to my condo on Front Beach saw the huge storm surge coming and ran for their lives out the back of their home, to hang onto some giant old oaks until the water subsided. So many stories to hear and so many to tell.

My son David and daughter Jill helped a friend fix up a mobile home, and when she moved into it I was able to rent her house. It is unheated and not air-conditioned, but I was very glad to be there and settled. I had slept in many different places at this point; it is wonderful to have generous friends who still have their homes, but so good to have a place of my own again. This two-bedroom house now includes my grandson and his wife, all my belongings and those of my son David and his wife, so we are packed pretty full.

Going back to visit the condo seems like something I just had to do almost daily. The debris was gone within two months, a gigantic task. At one point there were 167 men and much equipment working to make some sense of the future of the condo community. After four months of inactivity, reconstruction has begun and the hope is that we will be moving back in this August.

Everyone has been wonderful to me. I had not been painting much for some time before the storm but have been painting nearly every day for a while now. I'm working on yupo paper, and perhaps post-traumatic stress is responsible for my erasing one area at a time that I don't like. This one could have been six or eight paintings, but I'll get there.

I've been thinking of a statement about having post-traumatic stress disorder followed by post-traumatic growth, and I'm setting my goal on that.

FINDING PEARLINGTON

LYN BAILEY   Pearlington

My husband and I are a volunteer foster home for the Ponchartrain Humane Society in Pearlington, Mississippi. We decided to stay and ride out the storm with ten of the dogs that we were taking care of. On the morning of the storm I was downstairs about 6 a.m., and I saw not a drop of water in the backyard. We thought that we were doing pretty good and patted ourselves on the back at how well we had done. Things were looking better than when we'd had tropical storms Isadore and Lily.

I was in the kitchen putting coffee on because we still had power. All of a sudden I heard water running behind me, and I saw water coming up fast out of the downdraft stove that is vented in the floor. I looked up at the glass doors and saw water three feet deep pushing up against the doors. I hollered at my husband, Sam, that "we had better get upstairs quick." I grabbed the one dog that was still downstairs because we didn't have a crate for him, and before the words were barely even out of my mouth, the doors broke out of their hinges and all hell broke loose. The water started filling up the house.

I figured that if the water didn't kill us then the furniture would, because it was flying all around like tops. We figured the furniture just might even trap us. We managed somehow to get up the staircase, and so we rode out the rest of the storm on the second floor of our house.

The morning after the storm, I was rinsing out our underwear in the bathroom sink upstairs and hanging them off the railing. I heard the sound of a chopper coming lower and lower, and I thought it was going to land on the roof! I looked out the window, and they were putting a rescue swimmer in an orange suit out in the backyard on a cord, so I sent my husband out to talk with him.

The man said, "Where am I?" And Sam said, "This is 6030 Gin Road!" And he said, "No, what town am I in?" And I said, "Pearlington, Mississippi!" And he said, "Well, you are not on any military maps at all!" Then he showed Sam the map and said, "The only reason we found you is because we were sent to patrol the Pearl River for survivors and we saw your underwear hanging out on the railing!" And then he said, "We are going to radio it in because none of the military even knows about this town!" And they radioed it in that they had found Pearlington, Mississippi. The next afternoon an army Chinook helicopter landed behind the fire station in Pearlington with water and MREs, and that was the first help that Pearlington got after the storm.

As I told my husband, "So much for my mama's old saying, 'Don't air out your dirty laundry.'" It was my husband's wild-print boxers and my white bloomers that attracted the Coast Guard rescue swimmers!

OH LORD, THEY'RE NOT GOING TO MAKE IT

COOKIE BELLO   Pearlington

We had ridden out storms seven times before Katrina. This time it was with my husband, Claude, his brother and his wife, their eight-week-old baby, and their eighty-five-year-old friend. Also, our son and his girlfriend and her mother, and a man named James from down the road. He had nowhere to go either. So, we stayed together. We couldn't go anywhere because we didn't have any money. We tried going to the test site but they turned us away, so we came on back to our neighbors' house. They had evacuated, but said we could stay there to ride it out if we needed to.

We were standing on their porch, thinking it was not going to be so bad. Then we saw the water start to come up in the yard. The men decided to move our vehicles up to the firehouse, since it was on higher ground. When they came back they told us that the back part of our trailer had blown away. And then things started getting really bad. Our neighbor who had evacuated, and whose house we were in, called us on his cell phone and wanted to know how we were doing. We told him that the water had been in the street, then in the yard, and now was up to the porch. He thought we were lying to him. We heard him say to his wife over the phone, "Nancy, my God, we have water on our porch!" and I heard his wife say, "Oh Lord, they're not going to make it!" We didn't know the hurricane hadn't yet made landfall. We thought we were in the storm at this time. Our neighbor asked us if we could leave Pearlington. We said no, because by now our vehicles had floated off. He told us that Katrina was still fifty-eight miles from making landfall and that the Pearl River, where we were, was at the center of the eye of the storm.

When I hung up the phone, the water was knee deep. Claude asked us all to start coming up the stairs to the attic. I was the last one, and as I looked out the window, the waves were over the treetops in the distance. I said, "Oh my God, oh my God!" We realized that we weren't going to make it upstairs. We could see everything blowing away. We thought when we saw that thirty-foot wall of water coming our way it was over for us. About that time, the wave hit the house. Took the porch right off and broke all the doors in. The water rode up to the ceiling and on into the attic. We had managed to get on up the stairs and into the attic ourselves. The house is on three blocks and has nine-foot ceilings. There was a foot of water over the eaves of the roof, and the attic floor began to give way. All of us women were screaming, and the baby was crying, too.

The men kicked the window out on the leeward side, and the women got out onto the roof. But we couldn't hold on, so we came back into the attic. Claude went out the window and dove off the roof to go look for a boat. He told me later that he swam over to our place to look for one of our boats, but they had all floated off. He was hanging onto a limb in the top of a pecan tree. He could hear another neighbor yelling something from his roof. "A boat! A boat!" Suddenly he saw a sixteen-foot Boston Whaler floating by through the trees. He was able to throw his legs over and get into the boat. The neighbor swam over, and together, when the wind would lay, they moved the boat from tree limb to tree limb until they made it back to the roof of the house where we were.

Right behind the house was an old CB antenna, and they held on to that to keep the boat there. They said for us to get in the boat. We sent the baby down to the boat in a Tupperware container. They caught the baby and managed to put him safely in the boat, and then all of us scrambled down and got into the boat, too. It wound up being nine adults and a baby in that sixteen-foot boat. It had no plug and was filling up with water. Claude and the neighbor continued to hold on to the CB pole for about eight hours in winds of 180 miles per hour. Waves kept coming and beating the house. We continued to hold on with everything being blown away and oh, the waves! They were so strong!

Finally we were in the eye of the storm, and it seemed to last a long time. The wind was calm, and nothing was moving. And then we caught the other side of the storm. The wind started blowing really hard again, and then it was raining. We had figured that once we got to the other side of the storm the water would drop quickly, but it didn't. Claude and the men kept trying to keep the boat from going underneath the eaves of the house. They decided to try to get the boat around the house so that we could get back in the attic when the water finally started to go down. It was getting darker and darker, and the waves were still big and the wind was blowing so hard. As the men were moving the boat around the house, so we could get back inside, a huge wave came and tipped the boat over onto its side. It threw the baby, in the Tupperware container, out of the boat! My daughter-in-law reached out and grabbed the baby and put him back into the boat! One by one we went back inside the attic, and we really had to watch our step because the floorboards had been washed apart.

The water continued to go down, and finally when it was low enough the men left to go find us a place to stay. Of course, the entire house was soaked and torn up, and we didn't have anything to eat, but we did have the baby's food.

It was nighttime by then, and when the men couldn't find anybody they went to the fire station. There was another couple there who had floated up in their boat during the storm. At the station they found one tanker that was inside and full of water. They hooked up the hose to the tanker and washed the mud out of the firehouse, and we all went there. There was a little section upstairs that hadn't gotten wet, so we all piled up there. The floor was hard, but at least it was dry and better than nothing.

The men went to check on things the next morning, and saw that the community center and post office were destroyed and the Catholic church was sitting in the middle of the street. When they got down the road a little further, they saw their first casualty. An old lady was pulling a boat, and her husband was deceased and inside the boat because he had drowned. They continued on and found that everyone's homes from the family had been damaged and had floated off their foundations. Everything was covered in thick mud.

We were all so hungry, and there was absolutely nothing to eat. Claude and one of the other men went looking for food. They started opening refrigerators. On about the nineteenth try, they felt cool air on their faces and found a bag full of peeled shrimp, a bag of roast beef, and a three-pound bag of uncooked hamburger meat. We had a propane bottle and a burner, and we set up an old barbeque pit and lit the propane under it. We didn't have any utensils, so we used sticks to cook with. We cooked the hamburger on a refrigerator tray, and it was just so tasty!

There were fifteen or twenty of us staying at the fire station. The next day, more people who had stayed behind started coming to the fire station for help. None of us knew what to do. We took turns hosing off with the fire hose, because the tank still had water, and that's how we bathed for five or six days. We continued on like this, hoping that someone would come along and find us. I saw helicopters flying over, and I was waving my arms, but they didn't see me. I thought this must be what it's like to be stranded on a desert island.

All of the potted meat and crackers were gone. The baby food was gone, and we were down to the very last diaper. Finally, on the morning of the fifth day, we heard a chain saw running. Claude said, "Listen, someone is trying to cut their way in!" and he and another guy started crawling over timbers to get to those people with the chain saws out on 604. It was the Tupelo, Mississippi, wildlife and fisheries game wardens. They had water and bags of ice they had brought in. After five or six days the military started dropping MREs and water from helicopters.

Once the military people started coming in we said, "Thank you, Lord!" It was such a blessing to see them. We want to say a big thanks to the army guys and the navy and Coast Guard and especially the church groups that came in and brought food and clothing. They were the best help of all. The churches are still helping people out and rebuilding their homes. It's wonderful what they have meant to all of us; they have opened their hearts and their pocketbooks, too. We stayed in a tent for almost a month. People were so good to us and kept asking what we needed. I always said, "We need a house!" Hopefully I will get one again one day.

You never know what might happen with a storm like this until you are in it. I know if there is another storm, I'm leaving. I won't go through it again.

STILL A HOUSE . . .

PAT PINSON   Ocean Springs

We turned down Halstead Avenue in Ocean Springs, heading toward the beach, avoiding the larger branches, and driving over a thick carpet of leaves and twigs. Already by 9 a.m. on the morning after, several trees had been cut away to clear a lane for driving. The sun blazed out of a cerulean blue sky and a crystalline atmosphere, so often the case following a fierce storm. The prevailing sound was of chain saws in an otherwise ethereal calm.

Friends were driving us home from where we had taken shelter from the storm. Our car had been covered with water, as had thirty-nine others in the parking lot of the motel in Pascagoula—our usually safe hideaway from hurricanes, located six miles north of the beach and tucked in a little dip that secluded us from the winds. Our friends, Corky and Marilyn, had already determined the fate of their home, and knew that there was nothing left of their house but the slab. This bald statement had echoed among other friends staying in the same motel—several more had nothing left but a slab. Someone had already made the trip to check Beach Boulevard in Pascagoula, and the report from there brought on a sort of stunned numbness.

And now we headed toward the beach in Ocean Springs. The road became more difficult the further we went, and finally we came to a stop in front of a large live oak lying in front of the pickup ahead of us. Unusual for a live oak to be down—they seem to bend with the wind. We got out with our two cat carriers and our dog, to go forward on foot. Two fellows were cutting through the upper trunk, and in a moment we were able to drive around it. A man asked where we were going. "That's our street there—the next one on the little rise—Temple Terrace." "Well, you can probably get there, but not beyond, there's a house across the road." The road beyond was also a sea of green and brown trunks instead of visible concrete. Our next-door neighbor came toward us. "You've got some damage, but it's standing," he said. Maybe good news.

We turned onto our street and were able to get most of the way into the cul-de-sac where our house sat at the end. We could see that all the houses on our street were standing, being on the highest point back from the water. The house was there but hard to get to. There was a tree across the driveway. I could see into our attic through a large hole, and the sides of the house were impassable. The hollow raccoon tree lay broken in mid trunk. I looked up for our tall, old pines. I always went out to bid them to hold fast before a storm—and they had. Only the top of one was out.

The yard was full of insulation, tree limbs, and nails. Through the front door, we could see everything still covered with heavy plastic in case the wind destroyed part of the roof. We knew we were safe from the rising water, as our back porch dropped some twenty feet down to the ground, which dropped again to the marsh that separated us from the Gulf Islands Park. Opening the door, Corky, an engineer, strode in, looked around, and declared, "It's structurally sound. You will be okay." The sopping rug underfoot had leaf pieces and forest dirt on it, the floor lamps were turned over, the books and all the pictures I put on the floor for safekeeping were wet. The cats picked each foot up and shook it as they moved, but we knew we were among the lucky ones, as there was still a house on our slab.

Kim's Story

THAOU THI (KIM) PHAM   Ocean Springs

Translated from Vietnamese by Lanna Mai

The storm arrived.

Around 6 o'clock in the morning, the wind blew stronger by the minute and the howling became louder and more terrifying. Rain poured down as if it were a waterfall. Within ten minutes, the houses adjacent to my sister's house had become little islands in a sea of water.

As we watched the houses behind ours, which were four feet lower, drowning in flooding water, panic set in. We had one thirteen-year-old boy and three younger girls ranging from eight to less than two years of age. How could all of us, five adults and four children, escape this ravaging flood, which was rising rapidly?

Then my sister's house began to leak in many places. Everyone ran around trying in vain to catch the leaks with buckets, pots, and pans; however, there were more leaks than we could catch. Outside, the wind howled louder as time went by. Glass windows, furniture, and the entire house shook violently and made deafening sounds as if the demons were let loose in an exorcist movie. The front and back doors sounded as if they were being beaten by a mob with sticks and were about to burst open. I felt like I was in a haunted house while demons were screaming and ravaging outside.

I checked my watch again. It was 7:30 in the morning. The rain seemed to let up a little bit, but the wind continued its terrifying roar. I felt that time just dragged. How slowly this hurricane passed! Everyone was exhausted from lack of sleep. How could we have slept when the wind kept blowing, trees and shrubs kept swaying dizzily, and some fences were tossed up and down countless times. I pulled out my cell phone and found it was still working. Thrilled, I called my sisters in Austin, Houston, and California to report our condition. After I hung up, I regretted being too chatty. With the power outage, how could I recharge the phone and have it ready when I needed it?

As I watched the candle flickering, sadness washed over me. I thought about my house with so many memories, which were gone with the wind. Katrina had destroyed the pictures of my father, my three kids since they were babies, and my wedding. Tears rolled down my face suddenly. I looked at my watch. It was only 8 o'clock at night, yet it felt very late. The whole family was sound asleep. How this day felt like a century!

The day after the storm, I woke up and looked at my watch. It was only 5 o'clock in the morning. My husband lay next to me breathing laboriously. My poor husband was tired, drowned in anxiety and sorrow. He woke up an hour later. I talked him into driving us around to check things out. We would go crazy sitting at home all day.

We went to our liquor store, removed all the boards. I was thrilled to see that the store was intact. It would not help me any no matter how many tears I shed mourning the loss of my home, my nail parlor, and my restaurants. I could not wait for help but had to help myself. There is a silver lining in every dark cloud. I decided to open the liquor store for business. I felt luckier than most. Happiness to me is to be alive and still have a business so that I can make a living.

It was curfew time, and it was a miracle that my liquor store still had running water. My sister and I were so happy. We ran to the back of the store to shower ourselves with our clothes on. It reminded me of the time we were in the refugee camp in the Terempa island in Indonesia. Our little hut then had no showering area, so my sisters and I had to wrap ourselves in sarongs and take our baths in a creek. Our current situation was no different from that in the refugee camp. Even though water made our clothes cling to our bodies uncomfortably, there was no worry that someone would walk in on us, since the back of the store was deserted. I reminisced about how I had enjoyed frolicking with friends in the rain for hours when I was very young and living in Thu Duc, Vietnam. After showering, we went to the restroom to strip down, wring the water out of our clothes, and put them back on, as we had no others to change into.

On the afternoon of the second day after the storm, everyone in the house was happy to see me bringing home a cooler full of ice. I felt very good about my modest contribution. My sister's sister-in-law put some ice in a small cooler to hold the milk for her baby. I watched her like a hawk, even though I did offer her the ice, worrying that there was not enough left for everyone else in the house. How selfish of me! Please forgive me, since that was just normal female behavior. Ice was worth more than gold at the moment.

THE WATER JUST KEPT RISING

KATHY BLAZER   Gautier

We watched the water filling in the empty lot next to our house.

The rain continued to fall as the water overflowed into our yard.

The storm surge pushed water from the bayou and connected to the water already overflowing into our yard. We watched as the water moved over our patio and then up the steps into our house. The winds pushed the water closer and closer, until the water reached into our home.

We panicked and tried to put towels under the doors to stop the water from coming in, but this was useless.

We went to the garage to get mops and buckets to try to move the water, but opening the door to the garage emptied the two feet of water waiting for us on the other side.

We stood in silence for a moment, sickened to see that our home was filling with water, sick to see that the dream we had of coming to Mississippi was now turning into a nightmare.

And then the waters started to recede. Immediately we began to move the water from the house, pushing it out with mops and buckets—the muddy, ugly water that had taken over our home.

Evidence of the invasion remained in the carpeted rooms and in the muddy film on all the tiled surfaces in our home, but the worst seemed to be over, at least for the moment. The winds howled and continued for what seemed like hours, as we watched shingles blowing off the roof and our lanai crash before our eyes.

Now for the cleanup, as we survived Katrina.

ALL AT SEA

MICHELLE DRANE SMITH   Pass Christian

We lost two houses. One was completely smashed and twisted off the foundation, and the other was reduced to a slab with two pieces of plumbing on it. We were overjoyed to recover all seven of our beloved bronze busts. Four of them were lying in the mud in the wreckage of our home, and three of them were in the unbelievable debris/wreckage of Twin Oaks, a huge assisted living facility, that had been reduced to eight columns and vast amounts of rubble. Amazingly, the only damage to the bronzes was to the patina—no scratches or dents. Five of my favorite paintings were also hanging in Twin Oaks and are also gone with the wind. At the moment, four of the portrait busts are arranged on the porch of a friend in Pass Christian. They look rather like they're having a tea party.

As to our plans for the future, we are simply trying to chill out in our FEMA trailer, which is a bit snug at approximately nine feet by thirty feet. I pretend that it is a nonpointy, nonfloating boat, and that helps. We hung lovely wind chimes in a nearby tree, and they remind us of the very pleasant sound of rigging in the wind. It is likely that we will move a few miles north of Pass Christian so that we can continue to enjoy those things that we loved so much about our former home.

ON THE ROAD AGAIN

MARJORIE BUTTERWORTH   Pass Christian

September 10, 2005: Just wanted you to know that we are alive and well and my family is all accounted for. We evacuated from Pass Christian to a motel in Diamondhead to ride out the storm, and that is a story in itself. By the time Katrina passed through there was no second floor, and water was dripping through the ceiling of our room on the first floor.

We left the following morning and drove to Florida for a few days and then headed to Houston to stay with our kids. A week after the storm we drove to the Pass to see how our new house of four months had fared. What a shock. We are approximately two miles from the beach and still had water up to the ceiling. We could see the rafters in the attic. We had left a car in the garage and a boat on the side of the house. No house, no car, and no boat. I have shed tears in buckets, so I am now through crying. Bert and I will just start all over.

Through some miracle, when we went in the rear French doors the bottom of the credenza was lying on the steps and there was my good china and crystal! We retrieved all of my china and hosed down and washed everything five times. Found a few other belongings but all our family photos and pictures are gone. Our friends all lost their homes, and Pass Christian is a city of the past.

After we get with the insurance adjustor, we will drive to LA and visit more family. Yes, at ages seventy-three and seventy-four the Butterworths will become nomads for a while. I have no idea when we will get back to the coast—we are both feeling that we don't want to live in Pass Christian again—it will take years to build back that wonderful little town.

September 21, 2005: Well, here we go again, with Hurricane Rita, sister of Katrina. It looks like these things are following us—I wonder if they would follow us to North Dakota! We are in Houston and may or may not evacuate, either to Slidell or to San Antonio. If we decide to leave, it will probably be San Antonio because the Mexican food is better there.

THE MUSIC SLOWS

ELIZABETH D. SCHAFER Bay St. Louis

I am a painter of music, and now that the culture has been effectively washed away, my heart and soul are left empty and scared. I have been creating visual music for thirteen years. For me this area truly was my inspiration, as it is a melting pot of American-born music: jazz, blues, funk, gospel. My works are vibrant movements of this wonderful music.

As I watched the storm come ashore from my safe, distant location, the words from Don McLean's "American Pie" ran through my mind over and over, as he sings about the day the music died.

I am truly blessed, for although our home took on floodwaters, and over four hundred framed paintings were stacked on the floor, it was possible to save most of them. And although my studio was flooded, much was salvaged. I've lost a lot, but my talent was not stolen and I live to tell the tale.

If we are being tested, and I think we are, perhaps God would say the people are passing but the government is failing.

HEADING FOR HOME

OPAL SMITH   Pascagoula

Katrina. The name will always be etched in our minds.

When we realized that Hurricane Katrina was headed to Pascagoula, we boarded up, packed hurriedly, and headed east. Two days later we got a call in our hotel room in Panama City, Florida. "Opal, your house is gone," they said. As I gasped for breath I thought, "What do they mean, gone?" It couldn't be; my home was brick and solid and well built. I just could not fathom the idea. We grabbed the few things we had brought with us and started driving home.

If I were to try to tell you of the devastation on the Mississippi Gulf Coast and in my town of Pascagoula, I wouldn't know where to begin. Along the entire coastline it looks as though everything was put into a giant blender and pureed all together.

We lived on the beach, and when we arrived at the site of our home, we could not believe our eyes. A phrase came to my mind: *surreal displacement*. Most of the downstairs had been swept out and washed away: bricks, carpeting, furniture, my art studio, Gary's workshop, the double-car garage. The second and third floor of the house were badly damaged and teetered precariously on bare studs.

We tried to get to my children's and grandchildren's homes. Our daughter's home was totally destroyed, and the others had flooded badly. Gary's office flooded along with three cars and a boat that had been parked there for safekeeping—after all, it was supposed to be a no-flood zone.

It is now one week since Katrina's arrival in town. I am sitting on my sister-in-law's porch in Moss Point, watching the sun give birth to a new day. Despite the destruction surrounding me, I marvel as the sun rises, giving form to all that is out there. Never do I take for granted this miracle and the beauty of this wonderful world that God has provided for all of us. And as we all work together to mend the broken homes, broken families, broken hearts, I am reminded that without each other stretching out our hands, joining together, it would be impossible to keep the spirit of this great universe.

STILL STANDING

MARIA D. BAISIER   New Orleans

We are exhausted here, but we seem to buoy each other up. The kindness of strangers and their encouragement help bring a familial quality to this nightmare. It is soothing, in an odd way. And I am thankful. We are all thankful. I find myself walking up to National Guardsmen and saying, "Thank you for being here."

"You're welcome" is their polite response. They are on duty in what looks like the rubble of Baghdad, but there are no land mines or suicide bombers. We just appreciate them for all they do. They say we southerners are so nice, that we insist on repaying their kindnesses, and they are surprised at our generosity even in this destruction. We offer them the food we are cooking on outdoor grills. Sometimes they eat with us. We offer them water because they are hot from delivering to us that same water.

We invite them in from the scorching heat and chat about their hometowns in New York, Florida, Delaware, Georgia, Illinois, Pennsylvania, Kentucky, and Ohio. They are all bedrock Americans and they are sorry for our losses. They look into our eyes and they smile. Sometimes they see such sadness there that they cast their eyes away as if they are invading our private grief. They gently but firmly put us to bed early in the evening. There is a curfew in effect, and they calmly move us indoors away from any further harm.

This is an awful way to meet fellow Americans. I am usually in their states on my travels, and I look much better than I do at this time. For some reason my unmade face is a badge of honor just now. I am scrubbed and clean. I smile. But I don't much care how I look at this moment, and I know they don't either. We are still standing together through the destruction, and that is all that matters.

September 2005

Five American flags for patriotism

September 2005, Ocean Springs
Keesler Air Force Base servicemen
unloading MREs in church parking lot

November 2005, Biloxi
"Golden Fisherman" statue in front of destroyed bridge from Biloxi to Ocean Springs, Point Cadet (statue later stolen to be sold for scrap)

November 2005, Waveland

Gwen Impson standing by remains
of her home and her husband's
beloved El Camino

November 2005, Pascagoula
Italian cookbook impaled on a fence

November 2005

After the tidal surge

November 2005, Gulfport
First Baptist Church

November 2005, D'Iberville

Relief tents

November 2005, D'Iberville

Signs of survival, living in tents
and trailers

November 2005, Bay St. Louis
Laundry hanging outside trailer, Ruth
Thompson's FEMA home

November 2005, Pascagoula
Opal Smith in front of her home, uninhabitable after the storm and later demolished

November 2005, Waveland
Historic markers of appreciation and
gratitude to all who helped in recovery
after Camille

November 2005, Ocean Springs
Mother and child repairing a home

November 2005, Waveland
Mother and child gathering belongings

November 2005, Bay St. Louis
Christ Church on the waterfront. Services
are held under a tent in the parking lot.

November 2005, D'Iberville
Stray dogs collected and being cared for
in a kennel beside a FEMA trailer

November 2005, Ocean Springs
Patt Odom

November 2005, Ocean Springs
Kristin Byrd gazing at pottery in her
wrecked studio

November 2005, Long Beach

November 2005, Ocean Springs

Interior of Shearwater Pottery

November 2005, Ocean Springs
Walter Anderson's grandsons, Peter Anderson and Jason Stebly, shoring up the foundation of Shearwater Pottery

November 2005, Pascagoula
Waterfront home proudly displaying
American flag

November 2005, Waveland

Woman standing by her FEMA trailer.
The posts are all that remain of her
home.

January 2006, Pascagoula

Waterfront home—all that is left

MIRROR, MIRROR: FACES AT LANDFALL

MARIA D. BAISIER   New Orleans

So many faces: smiling, caring, questioning. People meet and freely embrace one another here, because we are human beings who have suffered and survived and continue to suffer together. We open doors for one another, carry packages for one another, do what we can to help. Military people ask how they can assist us. And we answer with our eyes. We look into each other's eyes ignoring the rest of our selves. It is the eyes that say we are sorrowing. It is the eyes that say we can still manage to laugh. It is the eyes that jump in recognition of a friend found or a stray pet rescued. It is the eyes that weep with sadness or shimmer with delight. There is no dullness in the eyes here.

Our eyes glisten with the excitement of survival. Appearances don't matter. It is our combined humanity that matters. I have embraced many strangers who, like me, are happy to see another day. No one is ugly or outcast here. We see in our eyes that we are regathering our inner strength in order to rebuild ourselves. And our strengths differ.

Several days ago, a lady approached me in Wal-Mart. She was a beautiful, older southern woman with dewy pale skin. Our eyes met. She said simply, "I'm so tired. Aren't you tired?"

"Yes," I answered. "Disaster is tiring. Are you sleeping enough?"

She reached out for my hand, anxious for conversation. "Oh, I see you understand what I mean," she said. "I have no roof, but I'm living in my house because the walls stood. At night it's just eerie with no lights and no roof. And I'm worried about my nephew in New Orleans. He's a doctor at Children's Hospital, and I haven't heard from him. I hope he's safe. I *do* need sleep. But when I look at the destruction, I tell myself that it's only a roof. So many people have nothing. Oh, it's just so helpful to talk to you." She put her arms around me, and I suddenly felt I had done something useful for the day. I had appeared. I had listened.

Another day I was at the checkout again in Wal-Mart. The cashier was a very attractive black woman who had arrived in Biloxi from New York City in 1980 with her first husband. She launched into her story, and I told her I understood about first husbands. We laughed together as she told her anecdotes of husband number two and of an engagement ring she had just returned to candidate number three. Her home has remained safe in the storm, and she had taken in two white friends who had been left homeless. A few minutes later they appeared at her register and told her they were cooking dinner for her—fish on the grill since there is still no electricity and the freezers are defrosting. We spoke of New York and how anxious she had been to leave there and about how much happier she was in Biloxi. She was in no hurry for me to leave the checkout as there was no one in line. When I did leave, she gave me a quick hug and a huge smile. We agreed that this was a time for hugging. She was a special woman, and I'm glad I listened and that we made one another laugh.

KEEPING IN TOUCH

SALLY PFISTER   Mobile, Alabama

Having lived in Ocean Springs for ten years, we moved fifty miles east to Mobile, Alabama, in 2001. Transplanted northerners, we had been through a hurricane or two—a low Category 3 at most, and people said that was as much intensity as you would ever want to experience. Katrina was alarming from the very first, and weather forecasters were soon saying that "this is the big one."

We hunkered down and watched that Monday morning as Katrina started blowing. The areas close to the water suffered through the powerful storm surge, and downtown Mobile was badly flooded. The worst was over for us by late afternoon, and as we were at the far edge of the storm we had nothing more than a messy yard to deal with. Power was restored within twenty-four hours.

Slowly news of the unbelievable destruction began seeping in via cell phone, battery-operated radio, and word of mouth. Friends who had evacuated were anxious to return and wanted to know how the roads were. Somehow our location remained accessible by cell phone—sporadic but surprisingly effective. We became a kind of communication center and with each call picked up bits and pieces of information that we could pass on to others, hearing their news in return. A network quickly formed that was of comfort to us all.

The cavalry began arriving when the adult children of many dropped everything and came as quickly as they could, with friends and neighbors, to help their families. They came loaded with supplies, and with the strength and endurance to dig through the soggy, smelly, disgusting debris. They were looking for the missing pieces of their lives and finding them all too seldom.

WE KNEW THE DRILL . . .

BETTY SLAY BRADLEY   Hattiesburg

Having experienced Camille in 1969 and others along the way, we knew what to do: fill bathtubs with water, stock up on bottled water, canned goods, and batteries, and top off the gas tanks. When Katrina came our way that Monday morning, we watched as debris flew and the trees were whipped by the high winds. As soon as the storm moved on, our son and a friend were cutting up an enormous pine tree that sprawled across our yard. They teamed with others to clear a path through downed trees out to Highway 49. We gradually realized we had sustained heavy roof damage, and we joined the army of "blue roof" people.

We were without water for a week, power for two weeks, cable for four, and it took almost two months for telephone service to be restored. We were lucky to have a good-sized generator to share, and the gas grill was going steadily as we took turns cooking up everything in our freezers. News of the world was in short supply, as was gasoline. The gas lines were so long, and tempers grew short. The most dangerous time was before power was restored, with an alarming influx of strangers up to no good. There were lootings, burglaries, and shootings even with a strong police and military presence. A large, fenced outdoor "jail" was set up to handle the rougher element.

In direct contrast, church groups from all over the country arrived, helping with food, water, and clothing supplies, manning shelters and assisting in every possible way. As time goes on, our faith remains strong and resolute as we wait with everyone else for FEMA to make decisions, for resolution of insurance issues, and for life to return to some degree of normalcy.

Simple Pleasures

BETTY OSWALD   Pascagoula

I have always believed that beautiful music calms the soul. Whenever I felt tired or stressed, I turned to my piano to release that tension. For seven months now I have missed the simple pleasure of sitting at my Baldwin grand, ever since Katrina tore my piano from our living room and tossed it over on the next street, with the case embedded in mud. Since I often said that my piano was the one piece of furniture that I would not want to lose, I think it providential that I was shown what happened to the case . . . the *only* piece of furniture found from our home.

Several weeks later my husband was talking with a friend while waiting patiently to pick up mail from the post office. The friend, who lived a mile west of our home on the beach, mentioned that he had the top of a grand piano in his back yard. Incredibly, unbelievably, and yes, indeed, it turned out to be mine.

A dear friend from Utica, Mississippi, came and got the top from me and took it to her husband's workshop, where he is making piano-shaped plaques from it for our family members.

Before long I will have another piano to soothe my soul. A Katrina cannot destroy the spirit.

survivor guilt

PATT ODOM   Ocean Springs

My story is a little different from the norm. Mine is a story of guilt—survivor guilt.

While almost all my friends lost everything, my home and studio survived Katrina. I was not even there. I was teaching a class in North Carolina when the storm hit.

Before I left home, no hurricane was even predicted. I left all my belongings as they were. The school where I was teaching had little outside communication, so it was not until one of my students asked if I lived in Ocean Springs, Mississippi, that I heard of the horrible hurricane that had destroyed our beloved Gulf Coast.

I immediately got on the phone to learn as much as I could, which was not much. Soon after, I loaded my car with four gas cans, plenty of food and water for a month, plus my art supplies. I looked like Ma and Pa Kettle going home.

During the trip back home, I saw convoy upon convoy of National Guard and electrical linemen heading toward the coast. I stopped in Hattiesburg to check on my parents and purchase a generator. A week after the fact, I arrived home to find, wonder of wonders, my home still standing and my studio without water. I walked around for days saying, "Thank you, God. Thank you, God."

The yard was destroyed, and I needed a new fence, some windows, and roof repairs. The yard around the house looked as if a bomb had hit it. Debris was waist high. My first week back was spent like many other people's, cleaning out the refrigerator and freezer, cleaning the yard, cutting limbs and trees off the house. With the help of a friend, I was able to get two new roofs put on right away, one for my house and one for my studio. I was very fortunate.

It was then that I started hearing the horror stories from all my friends and learned how many of the art studios and galleries on the coast had been destroyed. That is when the survivor guilt and the resulting mixed emotions began. I was so happy for not losing everything, but at the same time, I was terribly sad for my friends who had. I was so grateful for my good fortune but grieved for the misfortune of so many of my friends and neighbors. My heart broke many times in those early days after the storm.

I met one friend who had been within a week of finishing a new home. He had lost his home and all his furnishings, his boat, his car, his truck—everything but the shirt on his back. He had just bought a small camper and had parked it in his son's restaurant parking area, but the police told him he could not park there. He had nowhere to go. I invited him to move it to my home, which he did. He plugged into my electricity and water and set up housekeeping in my front yard.

One evening we were cooking out and talking. I mentioned that I was going to add on to my studio when this was over. Since he was waiting on FEMA and insurance to settle and could not go anywhere or do anything until after that, he had nothing to do and offered to build it for cost. I took him up on that sweet offer. We started the very next day.

A few days later, I noticed a group of young men setting up tents and trailers across the street from my home. After a day or two one of the workers knocked on my door and asked if they could run a hose from my spigot across the street so they could shower in the evening. Of course I agreed and was glad to be doing something to ease my guilt. They started using my water each afternoon after they finished their work of picking up debris all over the front beach.

With a guilt so strong, I still felt I was not helping enough, so one afternoon when they finished their work, I walked across the street and told the foremen that I would be glad to wash their laundry since they were working so hard for Ocean Springs. I didn't hear from them for two days, until one evening a young boy about nineteen knocked on my door and politely asked, "Ms. Patt, did you mean what you said about washing clothes?" I laughed, said yes, and took his duffle bag, the first of many.

I was very proud of myself after that first load was clean and tidily packed into the duffle bag. (You must understand, I am a painter and a teacher. I am not fond of any household chores, nor am I particularly good at them.)

The next evening three duffle bags full of smelly, dirty clothes were waiting on my porch. I was about to start washing, when I realized there was no water pressure. That began a pattern in which I could not start washing until 10 or 11 at night. My personal bathing did not even start until well after midnight.

Pretty soon, I was shopping for Clorox and detergent every day and dealing with seven or eight loads of clothes nightly. This went on for about three months. My painting, which I was accustomed to doing every day, had taken a backseat to the business at hand: washing clothes. I became a washerwoman.

My fingers weathered, my job suffered, my late-night showers grew later, my eyes drooped further, and my money was spent on soapsuds, electricity, and water bills. The benefit was that I was happy doing what I could, and even though my energy was fading, my survivor guilt was fading faster.

I learned a very big lesson during this process. Life is like a boomerang. Whatever you give out and put into action is the very spirit that comes back to you tenfold. I found that my washerwoman activities turned out to be a highly effective way to deal with survivor guilt.

It seemed every time I did anything good or worthwhile, it came back to me in many ways. I was truly blessed while I was just trying to help others.

I can see now that my faith in humankind—and myself—was restored by this storm.

FRIENDS BECOME STRANGERS AND STRANGERS BECOME FRIENDS IN KATRINALAND

ANN GUICE   Biloxi

Maybe it is because Harry D. Reeks was an official Marine Corps combat artist who invaded Iwo Jima with the troops. Maybe it is because the artist saw life from a very different perspective than most of us ever will—or want to. Maybe it is because *The Golden Fisherman* is timeless, even faceless, but it was solid in spirit. Was *The Golden Fisherman* casting his net to sea to capture life or souls? The net looked lost in downtown Biloxi by the hospital—I had no idea what he was trying to catch there! When the city moved the statue to Point Cadet I celebrated, for now he would have a more proper setting for his image to shine—literally—as he cast to the sea and beckoned strangers to my city. He faced south and east welcoming each day and hailing the bountiful waters of life and fun. There were great debates about the artistic quality of this statue and on more than one occasion I defended his uniqueness and artistic strength. When it was rumored the statue was being moved, I wanted to buy it for my yard on the bayou. Thank goodness I didn't move him there, or *The Golden Fisherman* would have joined Neptune as a fishing buddy.

There is a quiet strength in the Mississippi Gulf Coast reflected in more than one statue. I've wondered if it is because we always heard

Mississippi was last that we tried harder at everything. I believe Mississippi is a world leader in cultural enrichment, too far from last to debate. We are like our own estuary system. We start off as minnows and continue to be enriched by our surroundings, moved by tides and winds and tossed by waves and storms. We mingle with so many elements of nature we are as much a gumbo as New Orleans.

One of the real joys of living in Mississippi and vacationing elsewhere is that people treat you like you are a foreigner, not an American. I used to take my two daughters-in-law to New York City once a year to absorb the colors, sounds, and flavors of the big city. Once, outside a theater, standing in falling snow, we were talking and laughing when a very distinguished gentleman approached us and asked if we "could say it." I could tell by the cashmere overcoat that he meant the comment as a compliment. Missy and Patti looked at me and wondered what he meant by the strange request. I knew. I smiled and said, "How are y'all doing?" He lit up brighter than the Rockefeller Center tree. He said he had been eavesdropping and was enthralled that people could be so happy. I told him everyone from the coast was happy. Yes, our culture is rich and we do smile and laugh a lot. Even now when the earth looks so brown, we laugh and tell people UPS is filming here and they wanted panoramic views. This gentleman would have easily spent the afternoon with us, but the songs of Abba were calling.

Friends make our lives fuller, deeper, and healthier. Who needs vitamins if you have friends? One of the most interesting Katrina side effects has been that our friends have become strangers and strangers have become friends. Most of my friends are living in different towns, cities, or states. I can't find addresses or phone numbers. And if you are displaced, you are not listed in the phone directory anyway. How do you have a phone if you don't have a home? I can't find many people, unless I work with them.

Or if you are lucky and a few friends have remained to rebuild, they are so busy clearing land, cleaning bricks, or finding treasures in rubble, they don't have time to have fun; and they don't have the energy. When you do talk, it's more of an emotional checkup than a conversation. There are no other topics of discussion. If insurance, adjuster, FEMA, or trailer is not in the conversation, you live on another planet. My friends have become strangers because everyone is trying to survive. And escape is not with each other. If you are weary, it's hard to be with someone wearier. The past becomes even more painful instead of being comforting.

Someone needs to be passing out psychology diplomas. There are government agencies that have hired local retired schoolteachers to go door to door just to say "hello." I'm not kidding. I have met them and they have official badges and pass out "help sheets." They ask a few questions, then go hide, fill out their questionnaire, and mark your home with a painted sign indicating the degree of emotional stability within! They have located all the bodies, now they are locating sense. Are these people friends? Some are if the questions are right.

Red Cross cooks are friends and Salvation Army volunteers are friends. The meals are not up to Emeril's standards, but it is pretty tasty. I almost ran into a huge hole driving home last week when I saw a house roof covered with men wearing black hats. The house was being rebuilt by another faith-based group of volunteers. No one will ever convince me government is better than family, volunteers, and neighbors. Are these people friends? They don't stay strangers too long.

I went to my first bank senior management meeting two weeks ago. I wore the most beautiful suit sent to me from a friend of a friend who lives in Philadelphia—Pennsylvania, not Mississippi. We have never met nor "talked." But she said she wanted me to feel good even if the surroundings weren't! Is she a friend?

My friend in Philly went to Tulane with me. We survived the MBA program commuting for eighteen months to New Orleans. He taught me much about business and people. Several weeks ago a box arrived at the bank. He had been collecting Shearwater pottery for years in the same desert sage glaze as I had. He said every time he looked in the cupboard he thought the pottery should be back in Ocean Springs where it belonged. I have not seen him in five years, but I feel his presence daily.

Harry Reeks had it right. *The Golden Fisherman* is not delicate or dainty. It is tough and strong, and he casts his net with determination. He is a fighter taking control of a battered and destroyed coast. The statue is plated and patchworked, adding strength to its huge size. It combines welds and lines with design and unique style. The Mississippi Gulf Coast is hardy, robust, and uncompromising. We will cast our net with equal determination. We won't wait for someone to repair and rebuild us. We will rebuild ourselves, because strangers became friends when our friends had to become strangers.

STUFF

ANN GUICE   Biloxi

They say, "Ann, you are okay. You saved your life and your family and Colonel. You only lost stuff." Well, that may be philosophically accurate, and I can understand what they mean. I give thanks every day that I have my life, my family, and my future. But folks, my stuff was great and it was *my stuff*. I never made a purchase without some reason, emotional, personal, or absurd. I have a story for every purchase. I can tell you about the fabulous ten-dollar pink vintage cocktail dress I wore to a banquet in New Orleans. I can tell you how many key chains I painted at night after the babies were asleep so I could buy an antique linen press. I painted key chains at thirty cents apiece for months to buy that incredible piece of mahogany, which I later filled with thirty-five years' worth of sweaters, scarves, shawls, beaded gowns, bags, gloves, etc. Not only can I not find the contents, but there is no sign of the linen press. I have looked in five yards and cannot find a single drawer.

I saved every Lincoln Log, every book, every Lego my boys played with. I had started a play collection for my grandchildren with my sons' old wooden blocks. I had every ornament my friends gave me. We always made ornaments for each other at Christmas rather than buy presents. I had the most wonderful Christmas tree with decades' worth of kids' school treasures, friends' gifts, etc. My holiday decorations would have never made *Southern Living*, but there was a lifetime of stories on each branch. All the toys and all the decorations—all that wonderful stuff is gone. No Nathan and Billy thumbprints, no smeared handprints, no clothespin reindeer, and no melted Mardi Gras bead stained-glass creations. So to say it is just stuff is like saying your child is just a kid.

Everyone has emotional attachments to their belongings, or the belongings wouldn't belong to you. The rocking chair that was Billy's great-grandmother's is not just a chair. What would you do if someone walked into your home and said you had a bunch of stuff?

I am getting over it. When I drove to work recently, the moon was setting over the bay on my right and the sun was rising over the sound on my left. I saw the shimmering reflections of both on the beautiful dark waters of my coast. It is such a gorgeous place, and when we rebuild it will be paradise again.

A FEW OF MY FAVORITE THINGS

ANN GUICE   Biloxi

As I started decorating and gathering furniture for my new apartment, I decided to visit my Gulf Hills home to gather flower pots and what few things I had found and left in the yard. When I arrived there, I met two friends who said, "Miss Ann, if you think there is anything left in that house, we will tear it apart to find whatever you want." I told them I knew in my gut I had dishes left in what was a kitchen, but I did not see how they could possibly get to them. The difference was that they wore steel-toe shoes, heavy clothes, and were armed with tools of mass destruction.

I had promised myself I would not go into the house again, as it was dangerous, foul, and had been condemned, as in "enter at your own risk," but in we went. We climbed over what remained of my break-front, stood on what I think was the dining room table, and walked on planks to the kitchen. I pointed to two corner cabinets. They started ripping up the rubble, moved aside some mysterious stuff, and pulled apart the cabinets. My friend Vince turned and smiled. "Is this what you are looking for?" He held up my green Shearwater bowl. Then he found two mugs, four goblets, a few plates and cups. From a complete dinner set of thirty-six and every serving piece Shearwater Pottery made over the last thirty-five years, I salvaged about twenty pieces of pottery.

Then they worked their way to the other corner and ripped open the cabinet and pulled out my Mardi Gras dishes and several champagne flutes! The meaning is clear. Enjoy life and drink champagne. As we handed the dishes carefully through the window, I finally cried. I was not crying for what I had lost. Instead I finally shed tears for what I had found.

WE WILL ENDURE

NANCY GUICE   Laurel

In Laurel, Jones County, my husband, John, and I were grateful to be sheltering family members who had evacuated from the Gulf Coast.

After Camille had taken away the family home on the gulf, his brother decided to build on Biloxi's Back Bay, where it would surely be safer. But when they heard that there were thirty-foot waves from Katrina surging their way inland, they all feared for the worst. And, of course, the very worst happened. When they returned to Biloxi there was only a slab where their beautiful home and all their family memories had been.

Jones County suffered devastating blows from the winds, and tornado activity was all around us. For nine hours, we endured the wind and listened to trees in every direction. My neighbor lost over 100 pine trees, and a family at the end of the street stopped counting at 450 pine trees. I learned later that many of my friends here had lost their homes. I could not believe this nightmare.

I hope that we in Mississippi will never endure this kind of hardship again. I pray daily for all those on the coast who lost so much. But we are resilient people in the South, and we will endure and come back stronger than ever. It has certainly brought us closer to each other and God.

ELEVATION

MARY HARDY   Ocean Springs

My husband is a captain in the Biloxi Fire Department and, of course, he had to be on duty as Katrina approached. He boarded up our windows two days in advance of the hurricane and left for work, with me having to do the rest of the hurricane preparation. During the storm, I stayed with my dad and stepmom at their house, which is near the high school in Ocean Springs. The house is over a hundred years old and had been through many hurricanes, so we felt safe. I would not leave the coast because I remember after Camille how hard it was for those who had evacuated to return. All the phone lines were down for weeks afterwards, and you could not get any information. Our son was in Tampa doing an internship, so I knew he was safe (but very unhappy that I wouldn't leave). But I was not going to take the chance of my husband and our extended family being here, and me not being able to get back to them after the storm.

We all came through it alive, although I did not know about my husband until the next day. His station is on Back Bay in Biloxi. The city did not allow them to move in enough time, and the water began to rise rapidly. Twenty people who lived in the area and did not evacuate literally came running to the fire station as the water was rising and lapping at their heels. My husband and his men had to put all twenty of them, including two babies, on top of the fire truck inside the garage, as it was the highest point. They then put up ladders to the top of the ceiling and hung axes on them in anticipation of the water rising and forcing them to go higher and having to chop holes in the roof and put the civilians up there. There was no room for the firefighters on top of the truck, so my husband and his men had to stay in the water for five hours! Luckily, the water never rose over the truck and the civilians were safe. I did not know if he was alive until he showed up on my dad's doorstep Tuesday morning looking like a drowned rat! I was never so happy to see anyone in my life. He is my hero. He was allowed to be off the rest of that day, and although I still cannot remember how we got there, we managed to get to East Biloxi. We found all of his family members; his mother and three brothers lost six homes, all completely gone. Luckily they all had evacuated to another brother's home in D'Iberville, a house that was brand new and finished just the week before. They all were okay. We then went to find my family members, and they all were fine, with very little damage.

Our house, in North Gulf Hills near Interstate 10, flooded with three feet of water! We are twenty-three feet above sea level and two streets over from a bayou inlet, and would never have imagined that any damage we would get from a hurricane would be from flooding!

My husband had to go back on duty and to work overtime. He had little to no time off to work on the salvage and repair of his own home. For two weeks, I was the only one there most of the time, trying to deal with the damage. Our son was still in Tampa trying to get through. Those two weeks were the most difficult of my life. I felt extremely overwhelmed and so alone. My husband had his own difficult issues to deal with as they were doing search and rescue trying to find bodies in the debris. I did my best to alleviate some stress for him. I worked from sunup to sundown pulling *everything* out of the house to either throw away or try to dry out and salvage. I would go over to my dad's house at night where they fed me and I slept.

The saddest thing for me was that all twenty-seven years of our family photos went underwater. In addition, I lost ninety-nine art books that were of great value to me. They had been very vital sources for my teaching and growth as an artist, and I had been collecting them for years. Some were autographed by the artists, and a good many of them were first editions and now out of print. In my studio I lost my own artwork, much of which was in progress for a solo show I was supposed to have at the University of Mississippi.

The college where I teach, the Jackson County campus of the Mississippi Gulf Coast Community College, started classes back up two and a half weeks after the storm. The students who were able to come back were so glad to be there and get a piece of their "normal" lives back. It felt good to be with them and to be able to help them "recover" in that sense.

My husband and I did almost all of the repairs ourselves, since all of our damage was from flooding. Like so many others, we had no flood insurance because we were not required to, as we were not in a flood zone. We therefore got little to no help from our insurance company. Fortunately, we had two bedrooms and a bath upstairs that were not damaged, and although we were advised not to, due to health hazards, we were able to live up there while we worked on repairs.

I have not gone anywhere (nor had time) to see the damage other than what is in my path from home to work and back, except for one day about a month after the storm. I was leaving my dad's house in Ocean Springs to go and work on our damaged home, and decided I'd take the longer route via the beach. I drove down East Beach, and by the time I got to Front Beach I had to pull over. I got physically sick. I was not prepared for what I saw. After that day, I just could not handle looking at any more.

My days since have been consumed with trying to continue my full-time routine of teaching and then coming home at night and working on home repairs, usually until 11 p.m. My path from home to school is via I-10, and therefore I see very little storm damage, which has given me somewhat of a way to cope.

The range of emotions has been *so overwhelming*. I feel guilt for lamenting about our loss, because at least we have something to repair and salvage when so many do not. I feel guilt in that I have been so consumed with work at school and work at home that I have not been able to go out in the community and help those who lost everything. Someone told me that what I feel is like a loss from the death of a loved one, that I am trying not to face it, and, until I do, the healing will not start. I guess I believe that. I know that part of the healing will be to go and see and grieve so I can get past it and move forward emotionally. I do not know if I am ready for that. I do know there is a deep urge now to make art and to put all of what I have and am experiencing in it, and I *am* ready for that.

My faith has been my refuge, and I know it will continue to help. God has given us a glorious spring. Things are growing, blooming, and giving us a sign that life can and does renew itself, and my spirit has been lifted.

THE WORLD THE DAY STOPPED

MARJIE GOWDY   Ocean Springs

It was the lichen that saved us.

The water rose in the blink of an eye. We shouldn't have been there, anyway, but I blame it on myself for not wanting to leave the house we had just renovated. So, we sat in the dusty attic peering through a window, my husband, my Pekingese, my cat, and I. We actually had left briefly, late on August 28, but turned around when we reached the interstate, as cars crept to the east. I slept in my new living room, fitfully, over the night leading to the 29th. We unplugged the television; the electricity would be off soon anyhow.

At 2 a.m., the winds picked up. At daylight, the bayou outside the new sunroom was rising. It was an eerie rising: leaves and tree limbs slowly coming up toward the windows. At 9 a.m., I looked out the front door. A wall of eight-foot waves was sweeping down the street toward our home from the neighbors' at the corner. That would be a wall: street, water, wall.

We fled to the attic. We all sat there in sheer terror. By about 10, as the whitecaps lapped just below the attic window, we realized that the house was going to stand but that it could shortly fill up with swamp water. My husband started looking for anything that floated: he settled

61

on two panel doors and two garbage cans for the pets. All of our life-jackets were on the boat, secured (we thought) a mile away. As Willard put the floatation devices together, the dog and I watched the swamp oaks six feet out the window. They are huge twin trees, each probably a hundred feet tall. Two hooks in the trees, meant for the Key West hammock, looked inviting as the first jumping-off place. Right beside the left hook was a large slice of white lichen. I had never noticed it before, but, boy, was I watching it now. The rising water slipped quickly up toward the lichen, covered half of it around 11 a.m., and then . . . then . . . could it be? Then . . . stopped. The water stopped. It didn't go up any further. Willard was still rummaging. The dog and I watched the lichen. (The cat could have cared less.) I didn't say anything. The water stayed halfway up the lichen till noon, then 1 p.m. Willard came back toward the window around 1, and I confessed about our vigil. Just as I told him, the water started to go down. And it went down fast. By 3, it was gone.

Yes, there was wind the entire time. Raging wind, first from the east, then from the west, howling tornadoes, limbs and large trees flying past—all of the usual hurricane events. But six-foot waves at the neighbors'? That made a big impression.

After the storm, everything was dark. It was extraordinarily hot. A few neighbors were around and began to come out of their houses. In our homes, feet and feet of thick bayou mud. Any remaining furniture, on its side and out the door. Everyone, however, was alive. By the next morning, I was feeling queasy, and Willard, with a heart condition, was wearing down. My son rode to the rescue from Tallahassee by the second night, through the kindness of the National Guard. Before my son arrived, however, I had a visitor: Holly Zinner, director of operations at our museum, the Ohr-O'Keefe Museum of Art in Biloxi. Holly and a staff member, Dina O'Sullivan, had ridden into Biloxi that afternoon. Holly was at my house to report that a casino sat on top of the museum, and the beloved Pleasant Reed House was gone. All of East Biloxi, in fact, was flattened. Holly told me to expect Hiroshima. She left; I tried to reach my mother in Virginia by cell phone. Just before dark on the second day, I was able to scream "Okay!" into the phone, and my parents could rest that night.

From that day forward, it is impossible to explain, unless you are here, the slow movement of time. The gradual unveiling of destruction. The creeping pace of your own cleaning of your own space. The unbearable sadness for everyone you know. It was week two when many of us began to see people we knew at the generator-powered Wal-Mart. It was week four when the arts organizations began to talk of repair and, perhaps, in the far future, recovery. It was two months before my husband and I walked half a block and saw where that wall of water had taken down an entire street of homes. There, we met an elderly couple who were beginning to pick up the remaining bricks and stack them; it is now March, and they are still stacking their bricks.

And it was after Christmas that the cities opened up U.S. 90 along the beachfront, and the grieving began anew.

There are wonderful signs of hope, however. They are signs all the more poignant and all the more important because they come forth after there is nothing. In the beginning, I went to the museum site daily. It was stark, white, quiet. In October, I heard a movement, looked up, and saw a bald eagle flying overhead. The eagles had lived at the barrier islands twelve miles to the south. They survived somehow and were looking for new nest sites. We have them at the museum—sixteen ancient live oaks, now sprouting new leaves. Homes for birds, protection for wounded souls.

Christmas brought decorations. Tinsel went up on FEMA trailers, and around the museum site, families lived in small pup tents, yet blew up huge plastic Santas in their front yards. The Santas are still there, defiant. In many cases, so are the tents.

Today is March 14, seven months after the storm. East Biloxi is still flattened, though there is commerce around the edges. Many people still have no answers. In my Ocean Springs house, the inside is clean again and fixed, the outside still wanting; the next-door neighbors' house has broken windows yet to be repaired by insurance. Many who were healthy before the storm are sick, yet many of us healed in un-expected ways, learning to enjoy the small butterflies, the glimpses of future that now appear.

It will be storm season again soon, and the season will come summer after summer. But most souls survived. The trees survived. Our futures are within our hearts and will begin once more.

AFTER THE STORM WAS OVER. . .

MARTHA MOSS   Gautier
and **DENA McKEE**   Moss Point

This week was "move back to the office" week. Parts of it are still not finished, but at least, and thankfully, the commode was installed. Had hoped the sinks and faucets would be finished yesterday, but no such luck.

The computer equipment seemed to have lost any desire to function properly, and the cordless keyboard and the printer were conspiring to drive me crazy. I decided to uninstall the software to the keyboard and then reinstall. This appeared to be the only solution. I tried it several times but to no avail. The software CD just would not reinstall the software. As I looked at the saltwater-stricken CD I noticed that it had spots. With no other alternative presenting itself, I washed the CD in the commode.

It worked and I was finally able to reinstall the software. Mission accomplished.

—Martha Moss

After a stint of four weeks with no Internet service because of Katrina, we were finally back up. We gave up on having phone service restored and went cable modem.

Our home and office were badly damaged, and we are temporarily residing in a twenty-seven-foot travel trailer in our front yard. It's not so bad. I've made room for my computer, as you can see. Don had a heart stent put in a couple of weeks ago and we have a new grandbaby as of Friday. Now on to reading the 273 e-mails that have backed up on us!

—Dena McKee

A LITTLE WATER

MELANIE MOORE   Pascagoula

Our house was completely washed away in Hurricane Katrina. The last thing I did before leaving the house was to put the ends of my silk curtains in plastic bags "in case we get a little water." Sometimes you just have to laugh.

We lived on Beach Boulevard in Pascagoula, in a house we built twenty years ago. It was moderately raised on concrete piers which had impressive footings. It was five thousand feet of solid construction, concrete siding, chock full of the stuff of thirty years of marriage and three sons, and protected by sturdy hurricane shutters.

I evacuated to my brother's house in Mobile with our youngest son, Michael, a senior at Pascagoula High School. My husband, a radiologist, set up camp in his little office at Singing River Hospital. And so it began.

On Monday afternoon the first report reached us. "All the houses on Beach Boulevard are gone and your house is gone, too." Obviously an exaggerated rumor. Pollyanna will wait for a more favorable report.

My husband, Hal, called. "Have you heard? Our house is gone." I was frustrated by these exaggerations at such an important time. I needed *facts*. "OK," I said, "now tell me what you *do* see." There was a quietness on the line that caused my heart rate to increase. Hal said, "Nothing. I see *no-thing*," and he hung onto the "th" for emphasis. I'm sure I've seen *no-thing* many times in my life, but I was having a hard time picturing it at my address.

I spent Tuesday contacting the insurance companies, listening to endless menus and recordings, being rerouted and bounced from one office to another, sometimes being disconnected and having to start all over again.

Wednesday my sister-in-law, Ann, made sandwiches and packed a cooler. Michael gathered work gloves, towels, and other supplies, and the three of us headed to Pascagoula. The ride to the south end of town was slow, as we were dodging debris and people walking in the streets. Two blocks from the beachfront the destruction was massive. There were homes missing, and even though there were plenty of people walking around they were all eerily quiet. It was very much like being at a funeral.

We drove to our yard and Hal was there. We just hugged and cried for a while. I was so sad for him and found it painfully unfair that a man would work diligently for thirty years and have the fruit of his labor disappear in a day. Hal's parents' home was destroyed, and his business office ruined. Our church was flooded, and we felt a great responsibility to help salvage things there, and help the staff locate members we had not heard from.

Hal came back to Mobile with us and the three of us lived with my precious brother and sister-in-law, Ann and Dan Reimer, for three weeks till we moved to a furnished apartment. They were our lifeboat. They provided us with everything we needed, and we will always be grateful.

September was a hard month. Many days Michael, Ann, Hal (on his days off), and I would drive to Pascagoula and excavate our yard. The heat was intense, the humidity stifling, the biting flies fierce, the odors disgusting, and the sights depressing. We would dig carefully for six or seven hours, extracting china plates, silverware, or a vase or statue. As there was no running water, we wrapped the muddy objects in newspaper and loaded them into the car. We spent the late afternoons spreading our plunder all over the Reimers' backyard, grouping like things together, washing off the mud and rewrapping them for storage. Friends and neighbors would often stop by and help or bring needed supplies such as packing crates or a hot meal.

In addition to scavenging, filling out insurance claims, and searching for more permanent housing, we had to make an important decision about Michael and school. It was his senior year and the days were slipping by. We enrolled him in St. Paul's Episcopal School in Mobile. He put on his new uniform, picked up his new books, and never had a negative thing to say. We so appreciate his courageous and positive spirit. He made new friends and earned a place on the headmaster's list.

Like many others, our first look at post-Katrina Pascagoula was a painful and shocking event. Even those of us who are not given to journaling found the need to sort our thoughts out on paper. During the first week of September I wrote the following in my prayer journal:

My house and all our things are gone and sometimes I question God. All my friends are scattered and struggling, our schools and churches are ruined, looters and vandals roam, businesses and banks are closed, and all of this goes on mile after mile, town after town, county after county. But I know that God is love. He is in charge and I need to be watching for how he is going to work something important through this.

Michael wrote an essay about his experience with Katrina. In part, this is what he wrote:

As soon as my mom, aunt and I pulled into our yard and saw my dad standing where our house once was, it all made perfect sense. Our house really was gone. I stumbled out of the car, all the while numb and awestruck. Only a few pieces of foundation survived. We did not believe such devastation could have occurred from a storm that was supposed to have struck New Orleans. Roaming through the mud and over piles of debris, we felt lost and did not know where to begin rebuilding our lives. With no other options, we began digging and raking to uncover what we could, treasuring each spoon and picture that we salvaged. That night I lay in my cousin's bed wondering how this had happened to us . . . Today I can say that Hurricane Katrina is the worst thing to happen to me, but I coped with it by staying positive and relying on the compassion of others. I will be a better person for living through this disaster. Truly, "'tis grace hath brought me safe thus far, and grace will lead me home."

And home we will go. Even though family, friends, and new Mobile acquaintances have all been wonderful to us, we miss our little corner of the world. We will build a new house and it will be stronger than the old one. We are stronger, too. Our faith is stronger, and our relationship with family and friends has a depth and a sweetness that can only come from sharing adversity. I can't wait to go home!

PROFOUND SHOCK

OPAL SMITH   Pascagoula

I sometimes lie awake in the night and think of the precious things that I have lost. All the family pictures, my favorite Bible, my pottery collection, and all my paintings. My studio was full of framed paintings. My spiritual art journals that I had kept for thirteen years are gone. I tried to write in them every day. They say that writing is the most personal form of prayer. Today I am writing and keeping journals again, giving thanks for all my blessings. We are safe, all of us. We are survivors and with God's help will come out on the other side, stronger and wiser.

It has been six months since Katrina arrived in town. Today as I sit and look back at all that has happened, I am reminded of my most profound memories of this time. As we first drove into town, people were already cleaning up and dragging rubble and debris to the street. It was so hot, so muddy, so humid, and there was a terrible stench in the air. But everyone was moving, doing, embracing one another, and accepting the challenge that lay before them.

As we adjusted to the shock of seeing our home barely standing, I remember thinking, "I can't hear the birds." There were no birds, no squirrels, no sound. The trees and other remaining vegetation were all brown, even the oak and pine trees. We lived in a sepia-tone environment.

Gary and I soon brought a trailer onto our lot. It was then we started looking for the green. Every morning when we awoke we went to the yard, wondering if any of our oaks would ever be green again. Two of them had had all the dirt washed away from the roots; one was leaning on what was left of the house, and all of them were leaning from the force of the storm. And then one morning we saw the green—the high oak in the backyard was the first one to come back.

Another profound shock was seeing neighbors' furniture, those who had some left, sitting on the street waiting for the debris trucks. My heart saddened. We have had great times visiting together on the furniture. I mourned their loss; in some ways it seemed greater than my own.

It was so hard to see the small houses scattered throughout the streets, with clothing hanging on the shrubbery to dry and mud being shoveled from people's homes. Everything they owned was destroyed, and my heart ached.

And then they came. Helping hands from many states: church families and church buses filled with kind people who wanted to help. The Red Cross and so many others that I cannot name them all. They were and are our angels.

We are living elsewhere for now, but I visit 1607 Beach Boulevard often. I walk through the front door and go from room to washed-out room, seeing in my mind's eye the way it once was.

March 2006, Bay St. Louis
Pearlie Goodman

March 2006, Biloxi

Thaou Thi (Kim) Pham standing on the slab where her home once stood

March 2006, Gautier
Yard signs advertising cleanup and repair
services

March 2006, Pascagoula
Group of workers cleaning out the
debris-filled swamp

March 2006, Pascagoula
U.S. Corps of Engineers employee looking at broken china plate at a home site. Patricia Mazzone (front) and Mary Jane Brown.

March 2006, Pascagoula
U.S. Corps of Engineers workers at house site. Shelley A. McDowell (front center), Patricia Mazzone (right), Deborah Harper (top), Mary Jane Brown (left).

March 2006, Bay St. Louis
Rosie McGowan taking the boards
off windows at family home place

March 2006, Pascagoula

Grandmother with her grandchildren
crabbing along the shoreline

March 2006, Bay St. Louis
Walker family sitting on an ancient and fallen tree in their yard. From left: Pearlie Goodman, Keiana Lock, Drea'Lock, Tatanisha Sims, Kecia Walker, Kadin Walker, KeShawn Lock, Glen Chilsom, Gary McGowan.

March 2006, Pascagoula
Children of a volunteer relief worker
come to help

March 2006, Bay St. Louis
Gary McGowan in front of the family
home place

March 2006

Unemployed young woman on the steps
of her FEMA trailer, smoking and passing
the time of day

March 2006, Bay St. Louis

Outside a play yard

March 2006, Biloxi
Bach Luu standing in front of a hotel that
was destroyed

March 2006, Biloxi
Phuong Trinh (Pearl) standing in the
rubble of one of her hotels

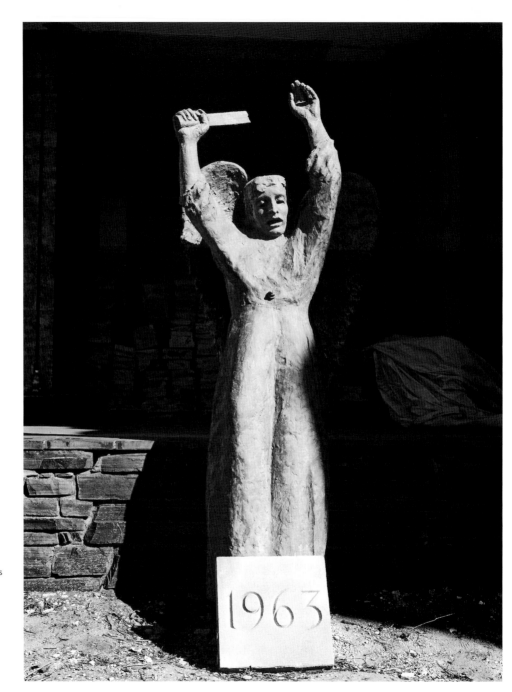

April 2006, Biloxi

St. Michael's Catholic Church, known as the "Fisherman's Church"

April 2006
Abandoned boat—"Do not crush, for sale, minor repairs"

Notice to Property Owner

This property may qualify for debris removal,
demolition, tree cutting, or other actions to reduce or
eliminate immediate threat to health and safety.
These actions may be executed by the Army Corp of
Engineers, however, to receive this assistance the
property owner must complete a **Right of Entry**
form. These forms are available at the Ocean Springs
City Hall at 1018 Porter Avenue, Building
Department.

Forms should be submitted to the City no later than:

Thursday, October 27, 2005.

If forms are not completed and submitted as required,
Public Assistance for this activity may not be available to
the property owner.

April 2006, Ocean Springs
Notice stapled to a tree for debris
removal

May 2006, Bay St. Louis
Ladner family in front of tent where their
home had been for forty-three years

May 2006, Bay St. Louis

Bobby Ladner, "Nothing was left . . ."

May 2006
Shrimp boat

May 2006

Shrimp boats

June 2006, Biloxi
Biloxi Lighthouse, established 1848 and still standing, with a statue of Pierre Le Moyne d'Iberville in foreground

June 2006, Pearlington

The Reverend Samuel M. Burton. He clung to the branch of a pecan tree with his Louisiana Catahoula hound "Lucky" for nine hours during the storm. His house was washed off its blocks by the tidal surge.

CAN THIS BE IT?

LOIS SWANEY   Holly Springs

I am the curator of the Marshall County Historical Museum in Holly Springs. We are a long way from the beach and were not critically affected by the hurricane. But we remembered that with Camille, some thirty-five years previously, the fortune teller Jean Dixon had prophesied that Mississippi would be blown away by a huge storm. This time, with every cloud, we wondered, "Is this it?"

The museum had been given an 1837 map of the city of Holly Springs. It was in need of repair, and we had sent it to Biloxi to a map repairer who said she would mend it if we wouldn't rush her. We agreed that we wouldn't. She began working on it and would contact us with progress reports every so often. After Katrina, we have heard nothing, so the 1837 map that had survived for 138 years was also the victim of Katrina.

COREY

MARTHA DUNN KIRKLEY   Columbus

He had stood in line with his grandfather outside the big white tent
. . . the one with a hand-lettered, cardboard sign propped on a rusty
old metal folding chair in front. It read, "Free Medical, 9 am to 5 pm,
Monday–Saturday; 1 pm to 5 pm, Sunday." The entrance—a flap of
canvas folded back and tied with a bungee cord—did not offer much
of a welcome. But inside, the smile of the volunteer behind the table
warmed up the ambience. "Hello. Please wash your hands, then sign in
here. Have you been here before?" went the mantra to each and every
person coming inside the thirty-by-sixty-foot clinic. This was Camp
Coast Care, in Long Beach, Mississippi, established by Jennifer Knight,
RN, and her volunteer friends following the devastation of Hurricane
Katrina six months before. Lutheran Episcopal Services in Mississippi
was funding the operation, and the donations of food and clothing
seemed never-ending. People from all over the United States, with every state represented at one time or another, had been coming to the
site. They gave a day, weekend, week, month, or months to the work
being done.

Free food, clothing, and medical care were offered seven days a week,
and some days there were two thousand people served. As Rev. Joe Rob-

inson, director of the camp, advised all new volunteer arrivals, "We may help or judge. We do not have time to do both." That perspective made it easier to open our hearts.

I was living in a rented RV on the property—sharing it with my daughter's best friend from college, Sarah. She was also spending a month volunteering at the relief center. I had responded to a call for mental health professionals, having a master's degree in counseling. Sarah had spent a long weekend with her college youth group from Ole Miss working at the center, and had returned after graduation to help further. Living in such a strong faith community was uplifting for both of us. We usually found something to giggle about in the evenings before we went to an early sleep, tired physically and emotionally from the day's experiences. There was such overwhelming destruction—so much loss, and so much pain.

The medical tent's records department consisted of card tables holding ten to fifteen file boxes stuffed with folders for every patient seen since September of 2005. Desk-chairs lined up in front of tables, with nurses seated on both sides taking blood pressure readings and medical histories of all who waited for the doctors. Three nurses performed triage for the two doctors on the opposite side of the tent.

The young boy I'd noticed sat down next to his grandfather, who filled out the inevitable but necessary paperwork. Corey was only eleven years old, yet there was more than annoyance at a hacking cough going on behind those big, brown, sad eyes. I had been working in the medical tent for about ten days, and had seen the depression, distress, and anxiety common to most of our patients. Corey was referred to me for counseling by the volunteer family practice physician, who had examined him. I introduced myself, and led him to my "office," which was two folding chairs facing each other behind an L-shaped half-wall.

"Tell me about your experience in the storm, Corey."

"I was with my mother and my aunt, and the water broke through the windows and broke down the walls."

"That must have been terrifying for you. How did you feel?

"Scared."

"What did you do?"

"We went to the upstairs, and the water came up there, too."

"How high did the water get?"

"Up to my knees. And most of my room got washed away."

"What did you lose from your room, Corey, that was most important to you?"

"My telescope, and microscope, and the worst was my autograph book collection."

"You miss your autographs the most. Whose autographs did you have, Corey?"

"All the wrestlers who my granddaddy had taken me to see—all the big stars."

Hoping to focus on something positive, I asked Corey what had been saved from his room. "Just a few video games" was the flat-toned reply. Still pursuing a silver lining, I asked if there was anything good that had come from the hurricane. The only response was a solemn expression punctuated with eye tics. A few seconds passed, and there was no answer from this bright, sad boy.

"At least no one in your family lost their life, Corey."

"No ma'am. My cousin and uncle died."

"I'm so sorry, Corey."

His speech was perfectly articulated, and judging from the things he lost from his room, I guessed that he was in the gifted program at his school, and that his studies were important to him. Failing to find something positive to focus on in his immediate reality, I decided to play to his imagination.

"If you could have anything in the world that you wanted, right this minute, what would it be, Corey?" Silence. Dead silence. More eye tics. Repeating, hoping for just a glimmer of a smile, I asked, "If you could have anything, anything in the world?" The long, painful pause continued.

Finally, he looked me straight in the eye, and said, "I wish that the hurricane had never happened."

I could offer no more immediate relief to Corey than he found in just telling his story. Maybe that small amount of "processing" would make the next retelling just a minuscule amount easier, I thought, as I handed his grandfather a referral to his school counselor, and looked up as another patient walked my way.

FLORA AND FAUNA

ANN ARLEDGE   Gautier

We boarded up and were in Olive Branch with our family long before Katrina came ashore. When we returned home a few days later the power was still off, which meant a freezer and refrigerator full of spoiled food, and the enervating heat and humidity of early September. Although our yard backs up to Mary Walker Bayou in Gautier, in the thirty-one years we've lived there we had never before been seriously threatened with rising water. This time it had invaded our home, enough that major repair work was needed.

It was fortuitous that we had moved John's fishing boat to higher ground in the front yard, as the boathouse was completely underwater. Most fortunate of all was the fact that the boat had a full tank of sixty gallons of gasoline. It took some doing, but John was finally able to persuade the boat's manufacturer to reveal to us how to bypass the tank's anti-siphoning device. With that, we were able to share the gasoline with many neighbors who used it to run generators, chain saws, and the like.

We hated to see that the extensive beds of daylilies that John has bred and nurtured for years were swamped and some ruined by the surge of salt water. The four raised beds made of wood and lined with plastic actually floated away. Some of our neighbors reported that it was an odd sight during the rising water. And along with our thinking about so many other everyday treasures of the Gulf Coast, we wondered where all the birds had gone and when, if ever, they would return.

Our belongings were piled into a series of large iron storage cubes in the front yard so that the contractor's repair crew had free access to the interior of the house. These iron boxes became a very familiar sight along the coast.

We collected John's eighty-three-year-old uncle, whose apartment complex had also flooded, and with determination and a bit of luck we found a place to stay in Orange Beach, Alabama, that would take us plus the other family members—our two dogs. An hour and a half away, this became home for several months as we commuted back and forth to check on progress.

The iron cubes are finally gone from the front yard. The fate of the glorious daylilies is still in question, although there are hopeful signs that a number of them did indeed survive. The birds have begun returning, and with new housing in place for the purple martins, these fabulous birds in particular are busily settling in. And so are we.

IT GETS A LITTLE BETTER EVERY DAY

MISSY BENNETT   Biloxi

That first day, after an arduous two-hour trip to the Edgewater Inn that normally takes ten minutes, we were greeted by the staff. Sixteen of them had stayed and ridden out the storm in the rear rooms of our hotel. There were hugs and shouts of joy, and, "Oh, my God! We're alive, and so fortunate!" There were tears at the sight of our hot water heaters rolling around the parking lot, and one of our signs in front of the synagogue down the street. The front wall of the hotel had collapsed, exposing the indoor pool and its cheery murals depicting tiki huts and island scenes. It was a strange feeling to look at our painted, imaginary aquarium and realize it had just actually been wave-washed.

I climbed alone to the third floor of the front building, the one closest to the beach, and looked back at the office and the main building. Its great, high roof trusses looked like a prehistoric animal, vertebrae exposed, genuflecting. My mind simply could not comprehend the enormity of the destruction wrought in such a few hours.

Our home had sustained only mild damage, save for the savage uprooting of massive twin oaks. Now the two-story white columns look like naked ladies exposed to the neighbors. But we are lucky. We still have neighbors.

At the hotel it is a different story. For twenty years, our business has been located in the heart of the tourism area of the Gulf Coast. At first, as we worked with forty-four laborers to pick up the debris that had washed in on us, we were aware only that our immediate neighbors had been annihilated. During my daily grieving session that consisted of reading our paper and crying, especially when reading the letters to the editor, I came upon an article about the mail. Our postman was pictured. The reporter was taking a ride with him and described the route as they drove out of the parking lot of the Edgewater Inn, "the only hotel left on the beach."

The enormity of that fact, "the only hotel," gripped me as I read it in black and white. I tried to comprehend that our industry was on its knees, telling myself, in an encouraging way, that the contract people, the first responders now in our rooms, are the new tourists. The fear remained that when they are gone, the other things tourism needs—more air flights, bridges, and moderately priced housing for the hotel and casino employees—will not be there, and a void will exist.

My emotions wavered between feelings of being very cut off and alone, even with everyone saying how lucky and blessed we were, to a part of me saying yes, but we have so far to go. Far, not just for our property, but for everyone in our industry. I had a tremendous urge to reach out and grab each of them and pull them along with us.

Our new guests, the first responders, the insurance adjusters, FEMA, and others, have taken such a proprietary interest in our rebuilding that they gave us a plaque. My staff hung it on the office wall. It reads: "Edgewater Inn—It Gets a Little Better Every Day." They said this so often that when they saw us light the buildings and the remaining trees for Christmas, I guess they decided to make that slogan permanent.

The days have all been like snowflakes, each completely different, yet accumulating to create a new scene. We are dealing with a totally different situation that would never have happened but for Katrina's wrath. I was amazed to realize the new furniture group I have chosen for the rebuilt rooms is called "Windswept Shores," and that a favorite paint color in those new rooms is called "Sea Salt."

We are rebuilding and reclaiming our inn one unit at a time, with a list of endless small tasks each day. My days and evenings are spent in line at Home Depot, Lowe's, Wal-Mart, and any other place where I can find accessories, art, and all the items needed to establish our "new" look. Things are slowly coming together to make us "normal" again.

I still cry out loud sometimes when driving on the beach from Pass Christian to Biloxi, but those times are fewer now. I don't cry as often when I read the letters to the editor, but I do take a fierce pride in our staff and their courage, and the hopefulness exhibited by everyone on the beautiful battered coast.

Seven months later the Indian hawthorn and roses are blooming at the back of the property, and near the middle, the crepe myrtles are putting out leaves. I am still rebuilding the pool area and courtyard, so their new plants will come later.

The procession of huge trucks hauling away debris has diminished, and in their place, concrete trucks bringing ready-mix and large flatbeds with building materials are coming to the many construction sites. Giant cranes are lifting our eyes to the sky and our buildings of tomorrow. As our past is hauled away, our future has begun tentatively sprouting, like the new leaves on our surviving trees.

It does get a little better every day. It really does.

CHALLENGES

KRISTIN BYRD   Ocean Springs

Katrina has challenged everyone. I mean everyone! Whether you lost everything, lost a lot, or lost only a few shingles, we all are changed. Katrina poured seven feet of water into our home. It tossed and destroyed all of our worldly possessions, including my painting and clay studios. The black cloud clung to us, but sometimes there is a silver lining.

The day after the hurricane, our twenty-year-old son, Colin, drove twelve hours from college to get to us with greatly needed supplies. What a treat to have Colin come through in a pinch. He has always been my settler, my challenger, so I call him That Child of Mine (TCOM).

After the seven feet of water left our house in shambles and uninhabitable, our neighbors and best friends graciously offered us a room with them. We stayed almost two months. Every few weekends my son would come home from college to help us tear out our house, our lives, our home, the only place he and his brother have ever lived. Things were not moving forward but were still mostly backward until Christmas break.

My husband and I are in our own trailer on our property, the kind where three is a crowd. When my boys came home for Christmas we cleaned up the attic/bedroom. Though it was sparsely furnished and had no heat, they still were glad to be home. Every day we tried to accomplish at least one thing, sometimes just sweeping around the bare studs. We had been waiting on our contractor for a long time.

Colin (TCOM) said he and his buddy could hang Sheetrock! They knew someone who was doing it and they just knew they could do it, too. Desperate, we said, "Start in the back bedroom and we'll see how you do." After deciding on insulation, using my hardware store account for charging *every tool known to man*, and buying gobs of Sheetrock at double the pre-K price, they were ready. He and several other young men hung Sheetrock for two days. Not bad, my husband said. Most every piece hung was straight. The pieces that weren't straight had to be done over, making those boys very unhappy. But perfection was my goal. After a few redos, they really started making our house look like it was coming back to life.

Then it was time for Colin to go back to college. The house was about half hung with Sheetrock, and there was still no contractor on the horizon. TCOM said he could finish our house. He had some big ideas of his own on how we could improve our home. After many hours of soul searching, we decided to let him stay home a semester to help us rebuild. That Child of Mine has finished hanging the Sheetrock and learned, from me, how to do the special mudwork needed for our home. We live in a house that was designed and built by a man named Carroll Ishee. There are a number of these houses and they are unique to Ocean Springs. Other friends who live in Ishee homes have come to see his handiwork, and they all want to get him to do theirs next.

He and his friend work on their own schedule; sometimes they start at noon and work into the night. But mostly they get up early, go to breakfast, work a few hours and go to lunch, work a few more hours and go to the lumber yard, eat again and work some more. My husband keeps me from becoming too frustrated.

Is TCOM changing his career path? Who knows. Does he love building? Yes! He has my visual acuity, which I got from my father who was a commercial builder all of his life. Every day is a challenge—sometimes with TCOM, sometimes with plumbers, electricians, flooring people, or window people. But the thing is, Colin, That Child of Mine, has come back to rescue me. I am grateful. He is my silver lining to this dark cloud.

SOUTHERN SOULS

KRISTIAN DAMBRINO   Grenada

Miss Mississippi 2005

August 29, 2005, marked twenty-four years of marital bliss for my mom and dad, and to top off a great anniversary day, Mom wanted Chinese food. So that rainy night in Grenada, Mississippi, she sent Dad out into the torrential downpour on a quest for wonton soup. Not only did he make it back home without the fortune cookies, but he also acquired a new hood ornament for my orange VW punch bug: a six-foot tree branch. When I saw my totaled car and drenched dad, I thought, "That wonton soup better be good." We ate by candlelight, though not by choice. By the time we were through I just wanted to find the way down the hall to my bedroom.

What I should have been doing was thanking the Lord I had a bedroom to stumble to. This realization struck me intensely when I toured the Mississippi Gulf Coast for the first time, two weeks after Hurricane Katrina. When I got out at "ground zero" with my dad, a lieutenant colonel in the Mississippi National Guard, I saw trees gnarled and broken, houses split apart on either side of a mangled train track, and one-hundred-year-old mansions that had been obliterated in just a few hours. Dressed in an army utility uniform, I flew with my dad in a Blackhawk helicopter over the entire Mississippi Gulf Coast. From the air, I saw eighteen-wheelers floating in the ocean like dead fish.

After we had flown over what was left of Beau Rivage and Casino Magic, Dad asked the pilot to fly us over Pascagoula. I saw Grandmama Kitty's home and her furniture in pieces on her front lawn, and I knew she didn't have a house to come home to. Her house was only one of seventy thousand homes in Mississippi that had been destroyed. I turned around and saw Dad give a tearful thumbs up to the pilot. I was glad when they turned me towards the ocean on the flight back to the army base, and all I could see for miles was the ocean.

When we landed, we drove to Waveland, Diamondhead, Kiln, Pass Christian, Bay St. Louis, and Pearlington. The latter was the town where we stopped. I got out and saw the worst of Katrina's destruction up close for the first time. Nothing was left. I stood on the foundation of a home on the beach and recognized the tiles on what I assumed had been the kitchen floor. They were the same tiles that are on our kitchen floor. This was someone's home, and a family had been here just hours before the storm came.

Driving to Jackson that night, I turned off the radio and tried to process what I had seen. I wanted to do something, but had no idea what to do. But when I woke up after a restless night, I started writing a song. I finished "Pearlington's Prayer" in an hour, and have been singing it around the state ever since.

I'm a town outside of Ocean Springs
Most people never heard of me
A picture of serenity 'til now
Pearlington is my name, you
Heard it on the nation's news
Hurricane did her abuse, and now

My train tracks are all twisted and
My houses have been lifted and
Security was shifted by the storm
But I still love the Mississippi breeze
Blowing through my bended trees
Bowing down as if to breathe a prayer
An old man stands beside his house
Nothing but foundation now
But a U.S. flag is draped upon his stairs
And he cries, "One nation under God
Bring back Pearlington"

She trampled on my dirty shore
Recklessly knocked down my doors
Screaming do not take your life for granted
She ripped apart my wooden floors
Where children played the night before
Now in its place a sign reads, "We'll be back"

My pictures have all blown away
My seagulls have all flown away
The priceless things I owned are petty now

CHORUS
'Cause the storm—she cleansed us with her rain
We've lost, but we have much to gain
My people persevere right through the pain
Hear the angels whispering my name,
"Pearlington, no one's to blame
God will slowly wash away this stain"

'Cause we are one nation under God
He'll bring back Pearlington
God bless Pearlington

Through American Family Radio, "Pearlington's Prayer" was heard by Gene Butterfield of Smith Mountain Lake, Virginia. His church had raised more than $125,000, and they wanted to adopt a town in Mississippi to help rebuild. They have been in Pearlington ever since. This example of unyielding kindness is only one of many that I have experienced during my year as Miss Mississippi 2005. I have seen people from all over the United States helping Mississippi, and they are still here for us. They have changed the way they think about Mississippi because they have witnessed our resilient spirits. Doris Roberts, who performed at the MSNBC Mississippi Rising hurricane relief concert in Oxford, said, "I am not a southerner, but my God, I think my soul is!" Hurricane Katrina made every American appreciate the heart and soul of our region. The survivors of Katrina have not given up on outside help and recovery, and neither has the rest of our nation. We are rebuilding together. We are all southerners when you get right down to it. Heart and soul.

SIGNS OF THE TIMES

MARY OTT DAVIDSON   Saucier

We live in Saucier, Mississippi, which is due north of Gulfport. It is far enough inland that we escaped the high water, though not the high winds, of Katrina. We are grateful that the damage we sustained was relatively light. A recent addition to our studio suffered no damage with the storm. Its new name is the Katrina Pavilion, and it is now a workplace for several three-dimensional artists who lost their own studios. Four members of my family lost their homes, and my husband's sister lost hers. But although Mississippi seems to be invisible to the national news, we are definitely surviving, and for most folks that means with few complaints and with many thanks.

I recently retired as a teacher and art gallery director at the Jefferson Davis campus of the Mississippi Gulf Coast Community College. I work in all media, but my greatest affinity is for wood and bronze casting. Two of my public bronze statues—*Pierre Le Moyne, Sieur d'Iberville*, located on Highway 90, just north of the Biloxi Lighthouse, and *Jean-Baptiste Le Moyne, Sieur de Bienville*, on Beach Boulevard in Bay St. Louis—are still standing. They are the only outdoor sculptures that were not toppled by Hurricane Katrina.

In December 2005, the first art show since the storm opened in downtown Gulfport. My husband, Ken, and I have three bronze pieces in the exhibition. There were lots of hugs and stories to tell during the evening. When we brought the sculptures to the gallery we drove along Beach Boulevard for the first time. Even though both of us were born and raised on the coast, at one point we had to stop and ask a National Guardsman where we were. There were no visible signs for us to recognize as we approached the town of Long Beach. It was mind-boggling.

SMALL BLESSINGS

PENNY SANFORD FIKES   Kilmichael

"One for sorrow, two for joy." Today I watched two birds fly in perfect unison, one directly behind the other, across a breathtaking rose and gold sky. The old wives' tale of inscrutable origin seemed a poignant reminder of the sorrow that had swallowed the Gulf Coast just five months before, and the glimpses of joy that were beginning to appear.

As a sculptress and painter, I looked at that symphony of color and clouds and mentally painted it, mixing my oils, thinking of the brushes I would choose to create the frothy clouds and iridescent swirls of color.

Five months before, I would surely have used raw umbers, oppressive ochre, and brooding blues to express the pain of seeing favorite historic sites and friends' homes reduced to toothpicks.

Perhaps it is the role of the artist to portray the overwhelming emotions of Hurricane Katrina on canvas or on paper or in sculpture. Throughout recorded history, artists have given us unique accounts of life's major struggles that convey the depth of emotions of the time.

Fellow Mississippi women artists will be inspired to record in art the destruction, the salvage, the decay, the restoration, and the rebuilding following Hurricane Katrina, and we must encourage each other to produce that art. It is our role to capture and convey the gravity of the time beyond the black and white limitations of words on paper.

What I see today are glimpses of joy, however fleeting, and progress, overwhelmed by the magnitude of the destruction.

At one stop today, an army of sparrows hopped in and out of a vine-covered wall, making the greenery appear to tremble. Their song was so loud, so strong, so promising. Elsewhere along the coast, the sound of birds has not returned, even five months later.

I cannot fathom how these fragile creatures survived Katrina or where they flew to escape her wrath. Will our human spirits be as resilient? Will our artists find their voices again in their respective media?

Just before dusk, at the gutted and crippled 1898 home of Admiral and Mrs. Jim Lisanby on Beach Boulevard in Pascagoula, my husband caught a glimpse of golden ribbon embedded in the ground. It was the ribbon to a piece of my porcelain sculpture that the First Lady of Mississippi had given Gladys Lisanby when she was honored with a Governor's Award for Excellence in the Arts in 2005.

Miraculously, after five months of heavy trucks and cleanup crews and even looters, the fragile ornament emerged from its earthy vault with no damage. My signature and the issue number were still as clear as the day I signed the piece. Even the ribbon maintained its crisp printing.

How had this delicate piece of art survived the savage storm surge of Hurricane Katrina, swirling in the angry water as the house was ripped board from board, only to be deposited unharmed in the sandy soil under so much debris? Finding that irreplaceable piece of sculpture and returning it to Mrs. Lisanby sent a flutter of joy across my heart like the bird that had briefly crossed the gilded sky earlier today.

Like that small porcelain ornament, the women artists of Mississippi will reemerge from the debris and will continue to tell the story of Hurricane Katrina with rich hues of emotion. We will find joy again, and our art will reflect the strength and confidence that is uniquely forged from surviving great disaster.

BRINGING LADDIE HOME

LOU FONTAINE   Pascagoula

Doug is sitting in his wheelchair, eyes half closed and head back. He seems to be going to sleep, but now he is snapping his fingers and whistling softly. Watching, I know he is calling his best pal, Aladdin, our nine-year-old sheltie. Doug's three children had given Aladdin to him as a birthday gift, and we quickly became a family of three.

A beautiful Shetland sheepdog, Laddie looks just like a smaller Lassie. He can run like the wind, catch any ball, and likes nothing better than lying on Doug's footstool while they both take a nap.

Now, due to Hurricane Katrina, we are all three of us displaced persons.

We are used to hurricanes. My husband, Doug, moved to the coast forty-nine years ago, and I moved there twenty-two years ago, the day before we were married. Unfortunately, forty-nine and twenty-two are not our current ages.

Our usual hurricane routine is to head for the La Font Inn, in Pascagoula, which Doug built in 1963. He was its only owner-manager until 1999, when he sold it and we retired. When it became obvious that Katrina was going to be a killer storm, Doug's oldest son offered to take Aladdin to his house and keep him while we went to La Font Inn. Laddie is in a wonderful place with a family of five to love him and another sheltie to play with.

We also are in a good place. We are in an apartment in a retirement community in West Mobile. It is spring and the lawns are green, the azaleas and dogwood trees are heavenly. Our apartment is pleasant, with French doors that we can open on a sunny day. Quite a contrast to the devastation that we see, feel, and smell in Pascagoula. But our apartment is not our home. And here we are not allowed to have pets.

People ask why I am working so hard to get our badly damaged house repaired. We didn't have flood insurance, so we are putting a lot of our savings into it, along with time, thought, frustration, disappointment, and prayers. But Pascagoula is our home, even if it is beaten down and on its knees right now. It will stand again. The saltwater-browned grass will be green again, and new azaleas will bloom in future springtimes.

If questioners could see Doug sitting in his wheelchair snapping his fingers and softly whistling for his pal Aladdin to come running, to jump up on his footstool so they could take their nap together, they would know—it isn't about the house! It's about getting the three of us together again. It's about family, and getting Laddie, Daddy, and me back home, our own home with all of its memories.

THE WAY WE WERE

MARJIE GOWDY   Ocean Springs

Biloxi, Mississippi, March 21, 2006—I drove the entire length of Harrison County yesterday for the first time. I had been focused until now on East Biloxi, beloved and devastated, and my sweet home on Davis Bayou outside of Ocean Springs. Let me stand witness to the swept landscape that is Gulfport, Long Beach, Pass Christian. Hancock County can only be more sorrowful, at the Pearl River where the storm shot in. We drove north, however, on Menge Avenue from the Pass and after a number of miles came upon what used to be and is once again as spring begins in this first year after the end of days: impossibly bright and large azalea blossoms, dogwoods, Spanish moss on light-green oak leaves, soft shadows rather than stark ones. There is hope, and there is remembrance now.

The Mississippi coast was a boomtown on the day before Katrina. More condos, more casinos, new attractions, new homes and subdivisions. We were all busy, stressed, traveling, on our cells, on our computers, commuting, at 7 a.m. meetings and 8 p.m. meetings, moving, shaking, doing it up right. Then quiet. Dead quiet. The din is beginning again, and with it promise of jobs and commerce. However, such descriptions could be made of any town anywhere that disaster had occurred. Along the Mississippi coastline, the vacuum sucked out by the evil breath of Katrina took with it, for just a while, the souls of people who really knew how to live. Let me tell you for just a minute about them.

They could cook.

Go to any neighborhood, any time of year, and remember that except for a few weeks in January, the sun would be out. Smell the fish frying, the steaks on the grill. Let's stick with the fish, and the shrimp. So fresh that it could almost talk. Tender as the night. Sweet as sugar. But spicy hot, too, of course.

They could tell some stories.

Soon as I moved here, the stories started. Neighbors would put a cooler in the truck and drive you around town explaining who does what, why, when, and usually where. Old women would remember their first fais do-do; old men would show you the two-step. Elvis rode horses through Gulf Hills. Al Capone and John Dillinger came here to summer. The wealthy left yellow fever behind in New Orleans. Histories were rich, and history was revered by one and all. Camille was the beginning of time. The islands were the goal, and everybody had something in their yard that could get you out there.

There were parties.

The good thing about parties here was that everybody was invited, and they lasted all night. The fancy ones, the Mardi Gras ones, the island ones, the river ones. There was a dress code: shorts, shirt, sometimes shoes, depending on your host. The wine was beer; the cheese was shrimp.

There was laughter.

Laughter on the dock, on the front porch, on the back porch, on the street. Waking up every morning to tell a tale, pull a prank. Laughing when we remembered who fell off the dinghy, who lost the biggest fish, and laughing in the face of wind and rain.

We laughed straight into the face of fate on August 29, 2005, and we cried till the tears hurt after the storm.

We'd be lying, in these months later, if we didn't admit that there isn't much to smile about right now. The pride's hurting a bit, and the outlook is spotty at times. But we're getting up every morning, and we drive down by the water. Down where the dock used to be. The sun's shining again, our souls are stirring. The water is shimmering. There must be shrimp somewhere out there . . . and the islands beckon.

CHRISTMAS IN KATRINALAND

ANN GUICE   Biloxi

I am so thankful Katrina spared my parents' home. I invited them to spend several days with me at Christmas. It would be different, to say the least. How do you decorate for Christmas when your collection of holiday treasures blew away or floated to the islands? My bayou home, complete with guest house, their prospective "retirement home," was gone.

Home is now a tiny attic apartment that I've decorated with the most fun stuff you can imagine. I spent less on the entire furnishings than I did for one linen press in my former home. I have grunged, junked, repaired, borrowed, and used donated furnishings to make this apartment a treasure. I think *Coastal Living* should feature it in an article on Katrina Chic!

This disaster has been such a series of out-of-control events that it boggles the senses. How do you make decisions with so much uncertainty? To date, one, but only one, of my neighbors is rebuilding. The coast has great plans, but the reality is that the citizens are weary and overwhelmed with too many choices to make and too little information to make them.

For three days this small family group enjoyed the simplicity that only a lava lamp, an aluminum tree, and other odds and ends can bring. The decorations were cold, but the emotions were warm and inspiring. It was one of the most memorable and meaningful holidays I've ever had.

THE NEW NORMAL

ANN GUICE   Biloxi

Some common expressions are appearing too frequently around town and in our offices. If I hear this is the "new normal" again I am going to slap the speaker. "Get used to the new normal." "This is our new normal." "We have to adjust to our new normal." There is absolutely nothing normal about what is going on here.

It is not normal for me to borrow anything. I'm the giver. I give to my favorite charities—time and money. I serve on community boards, foundation boards, and charity boards. I don't take from anyone. I give to everyone. It is not normal for me to wear three people's clothes at one time! Now you are sitting there wondering, why doesn't she get off her chair and go shopping? I tried. One of my best friends, an attorney, walked down to my office for coffee last week. She was still in jeans and an old shirt. She had lost her beautiful beach home, bay home, sailboat, and all belongings. Her daughter was to be married September 10 at the beach house, but obviously that did not happen. When she saw me in my borrowed clothes outfit, she rushed to hug me. We hugged and laughed at how ridiculous we looked. But this is amazing—we are both suffering from the same "illness." We can't go shopping to buy clothes. We are two professional women used to dressing for success, and we look like hippies who made bad design choices. She went to a conference in China with a carry-on containing two pairs of blue jeans and two shirts and returned with the same clothes—still in a carry-on bag. She could not shop. She could not buy clothes. I tried twice.

My sanity rule is to get the heck out of here every other weekend. I can only take so much; then I need green space, colorful flowers, landscaping, a tablecloth dinner, cocktail time, and nicer used clothes. You get the picture. So while I was in Florida, my friend took me to a wonderful shopping area in Destin. After a double latte, I thought I was ready to shop. I thought I could walk into a store and make decisions. Wrong. I sat paralyzed in the coffee shop, broke out in a cold sweat, and almost ran out of the store to tackle this woman walking by the window carrying six shopping bags. I wanted to rant and rave about excess. How could she behave so frivolously? How could she possibly need all that was in those bags? How could she not mix and match? I walked to the car with my concerned friend and decided I needed a drink rather than shopping.

Weeks later I drove to a wonderful new shopping area in Eastern Shore, Alabama. I could buy shoes, clothes, socks, and stockings, all in one trip. I don't even have a pair of stockings, so forget the good shoes! I'm still wearing sandals and jeans to the bank. I was thrilled with the adventure. I was psyched up and ready to burn plastic. I was going to treat myself to a special shopping extravaganza. I made it to the lingerie department and started looking at all the selections. I lasted fifteen minutes, stopped breathing, and headed for the car. I drove three hours, spent money on gas, and shopped for fifteen minutes.

A week later I tried a small boutique in downtown Ocean Springs. I bought fun, frivolous clothes I would have never even looked at pre-K. I was happier to spend my money locally, pay way too much, have too few choices, and still look like a wild child rather than a professional.

No, this is not normal.

WAR ZONE

ANN GUICE   Biloxi

If you remember where the lighthouse is in Biloxi, this will make sense. It is the only thing left standing until you come to the new police station on Howard Avenue. All the wonderful old homes, Moran's art studio, Russene's Antiques are all slabs—or parts of slabs. And they were on the high ridge of the Biloxi beach. Any giant oak still standing is dark brown and full of stuff that blows in the slight breeze.

Behind Nativity Elementary is a MASH unit. It is a volunteer unit with people from all over the country. I filled out the forms and waited with a group from Plaquemines Parish in Louisiana to get our required tetanus and hepatitis shots so we could return to the sites of our homes. My guy was nice and made sure the shots did not hurt.

It is so hot I don't know how those volunteers are dealing with it, especially inside the heavy canvas tents. It is surreal to be on a school yard and between the swing sets and slides are hospital tents, armed guards, patrols, jeeps, etc. In order to get back to work at the bank, we decided to take Highway 90. We had to go through two checkpoints. I find the uniforms and rifles very difficult to see. There are military landing craft in the Small Craft Harbor, and in front of the Church of the Redeemer is an army tent camp right on the beach. I was amazed at how much of the road has already been cleared of homes, cars, and so forth. I've been told that the barrier islands, Horn, Ship, and Cat, are totally littered with debris from the storm—the same homes, cars, animals, appliances that were lost here are now piled on the outer islands. That must be a sight. The Mississippi Sound is littered with livestock, and the deer are gone from Cat Island.

Almost all of the food is gone from the Peoples Bank "grocery store" we've set up in the Trust area. With thirty-four bank families completely homeless and most everyone else with some damage, limited supplies, and no access, shopping has been brisk. The Salvation Army has been incredible in providing hot meals to the people downtown. The helicopters keep flying over, and we were told there is a plan to hasten construction of the Biloxi–Ocean Springs bridge. Earlier today the only working bridge into Biloxi was stuck open. That means no one can go home. Maybe it will be fixed soon.

THE WEDDING IS ON

ANN GUICE   Biloxi

I went to a wedding at the Episcopal church in Ocean Springs. A good friend's son was being married. The church in Gulfport where the wedding was to take place had been destroyed, as was the Isle of Capri, the intended site of the reception.

The flowers were not the bride's first choice, but she had flowers. We worked all week on getting the word out that the wedding was on, and to come in whatever you owned—and people did. The prevailing attire was jeans and tennis shoes. But the young couple appreciated the effort, and they were delighted to be surrounded by friends.

The horror tales of escape, from my friends, left me breathless. The groom's family had stayed in their home only to be chased out as the waters rose; they waded back when it receded, only to find a house full of water moccasins. They escaped again and made it to Jackson after eight hours of driving on the wrong side of Highway 49, crossing back and forth as needed. The day was filled with tale after tale of people's determination and ability to survive.

A man I had just met is not from here. He stood amazed as friend after friend hugged and shared adventure stories. His comment was "I've never met people like this before in my life." I'm not sure if he meant we were all crazy for living on the water or what, but he was impressed.

I came to work today and again made it through the military checkpoints and the mountains of rubble to my desk. This is all that is normal. I received a call that my name has moved up on the list for a place to live, so I may be moving to higher ground. I hope no one thinks of any of this as a complaint. Life is what life is. I see lots of opportunities here, and each day is another adventure.

REGROUPING

GWEN IMPSON Bay St. Louis

I am a printmaker, art instructor, and president of The Arts, Hancock County. We have a wonderful, active arts colony here, and we all work very hard to keep it going and thriving. In the aftermath of the storm we set up shop in a makeshift office. Our immediate focus was on locating the two-hundred-plus members of the group, trying to bring them home, and helping them to rebuild their artistic lives. We developed an "adopt an artist" program so donors can give art supplies directly to a recipient in need. We also began working on a book showcasing our artists, whose work will form the core of a traveling exhibit.

By the end of October, two months after Katrina, Bay St. Louis resumed its popular Second Saturday art event. Though it was scaled back from three blocks of shops to just three shops, some four hundred people turned out. It was nice to get out, listen to music, have an art party, and connect with one another again. We decided to do it every Saturday, inspiring artists and visitors, and we have resumed our series of classes with subjects of interest to our artists.

We lived on a beautiful street in Waveland, half a block off the beach, on relatively high ground. We were told we didn't need flood insurance, but fortunately we had signed up for it anyway, prior to Katrina's onslaught. Our house is gone and we are living in a thirty-foot travel trailer in the driveway of a friend's gutted-out house.

Our daughter and son-in-law, whose home in Bay St. Louis was also gutted, bought a new washer and dryer, only to find that they wouldn't be able to use them in their currently unlivable house because the wiring needs to be reworked. The sparkling new washer and dryer are now installed in the friend's empty shell of a house, where the electricity somehow is working, and they are in constant use by grateful friends and neighbors.

JOSH

MARTHA DUNN KIRKLEY   Columbus

It was not unusual to open the free medical clinic under the big white tent and find seventy-five to one hundred people stoically waiting to be seen. Camp Coast Care, a hurricane relief center, could sleep and feed up to a hundred and fifty volunteers in a converted gymnasium borrowed from Coast Episcopal School in Long Beach. For those more comfortable camping out, there was space on the grounds reserved for tents.

It was chilly inside the tent on this January day, five months after Katrina ravaged the coast. Potential patients began streaming in, sitting in the long line of chair-desks to fill out their paperwork. Nurses were waiting to begin checking vital signs and taking medical histories.

I scanned the new group, looking to observe outward signs of stress and anxiety. My role was that of counselor, and after a week of working inside the tent I found I could often spot those needing someone to talk to, rather than waiting for a doctor's referral. The propane heater was lit now, and I moved closer to it to warm my hands. As I did, I noticed a man in his late twenties or early thirties, finishing up his medical history form. Judging by his physique, this young man was no stranger to manual labor, and he had a look of purpose on his face.

"Good morning." I smiled, looking into his clear, blue eyes, and sitting down in the empty chair beside him.

"Hey, how are you?" he automatically replied.

"Doin' well. Were you here for Katrina?" I asked.

"Oh, yeah. My wife and two kids evacuated a few miles north of here, and we were some of the lucky ones."

"How do you mean?"

"Well, our house was saved."

"You were luckier than most, for sure."

"We had a rental house that was a total loss, though. My brother and I are trying to work on it to get it livable again. Should take about six months. We both work on the Mississippi River, and getting time off is hard."

"Was he living in the rental house?"

"No, we had renters. A Vietnamese family of four—wife and husband and their two children—were living there."

"What happened to them?"

"We're putting them up somewhere else until we can fix the house they were in."

"You mean you are paying their rent for six months somewhere else?"

"Yeah. See, I thought that since the Lord saw fit to save my house, then I could pay to take care of another family that wasn't so blessed."

Deeply moved by this young man's compassion, I could only say, "You are truly a light in this world. Thank you." My next thought was that this was a story for CNN: how the depths of the human spirit can shine through, even in the face of mass destruction and overwhelming loss. In meeting someone who lived out his faith, I found that my belief in the goodness of people was reinforced that morning.

HOME AWAY FROM HOME

JEAN LANEY   Pascagoula

We had evacuated to Tupelo ahead of the storm. That's where our daughter and her family live—our "home away from home"—and we have the thought of retiring there one day. Although our house in Pascagoula is just a block from the beach, in the more than forty years we had lived there we had never been seriously threatened by rising water.

I had gone on to bed the night of August 29 when Bobby, my husband, got a call from a friend who had stayed behind. "Doesn't look good" was the message. It appeared that the storm surge had sent at least five feet of water through our home. Bobby kept the news to himself through a very long night. The next day or so we collected ourselves and drove to Pascagoula, along with family members and other kind friends who wanted to help.

We found a nightmare of tangled furniture, rugs, and belongings and began the backbreaking work of pulling everything out of the house, just as our neighbors were doing. There was also serious roof damage, and we joined the "blue roof" crowd in a hurry. At first we camped out with kind friends who had less damage than we did, but then we purchased an RV. The RV serves as yet another "home away from home," a secure place to stay while we make frequent visits to deal with paper-work and reconstruction.

When I carried an armload of salvaged clothing to a dry cleaner in Tupelo, the manager asked if by chance we had been affected by Katrina. I shared some of our recent experiences, and he was so kind and sympathetic. When I returned several days later to retrieve the clothing, he insisted there was no charge. At the same time Bobby had some work done on his truck and was also told "no charge." There were so many Mississippians anxious for the opportunity to help in whatever way they could.

LANGUAGE AND PSYCHOLOGY

KATHERINE LOCHRIDGE Pascagoula

A whole new vocabulary emerged, and it wasn't native to any of us: debris and debris removal . . . FEMA . . . adjusters . . . permits . . . corps of engineers . . . surge levels . . . relief workers. Almost as if by osmosis, everyone lost their old expressions and started to speak in this new language. It was learned on the streets and in driveways, as people shared intelligence and gossip about how to manage and how to cope. Initially, with no TV, radio, or newspapers, rumor and conversation were the only ways to gain and share information.

In addition to facing a storm that ravaged everyone's home, life, livelihood, we had lost our language as well. We were suddenly facing all of it with no guideposts. It wasn't just a question of street signs (though they, too, were gone, along with many of the actual streets), but we also missed the very anchors of the landscape. Where were the sites that told us where we were? We searched in vain for the places that were familiar, so familiar before—ones we hadn't really noticed or considered significant until they were gone. The disorientation and lack of grounding was profound, even among rock-solid individuals who are normally so steady.

Though I am not a psychologist or social scientist, it seems to me that Katrina put us all right at the bottom of Maslow's hierarchy of needs. Maslow suggests that we have needs ranked in a hierarchy, with physical ones (like hunger or thirst) at the bottom of a pyramid, and safety, belonging (like love or affiliations), self-esteem, and actualization continuing upward. It was his belief that until lower-level needs are satisfied, we can't move psychologically up the pyramid. With no running water or power, we were definitely on the bottom of the needs pyramid.

But back to language again. As time passed, we gained new words: rebuild . . . restore . . . and eventually . . . renew. With new words, another psychological term—displacement—took over. More hope and optimism came, not in waves, but in small wisps and breaths. When one more thing went right than went wrong in a given day, it was something to celebrate.

Much of the pain, chaos, and turmoil inflicted by Katrina, while certainly very real, started to smooth out gradually. Volunteers from around the country lifted our spirits and our houses, while all of our pitching in and hard work made everything look a little better each day. For me, the memory of the ruined books and scarred artworks dimmed a bit, and a dear friend's serious illness put Katrina's chaos into perspective. When positive and better days of hope and optimism began to displace those Katrina experiences, we had to acknowledge the blessing of displacement. What a surprising blessing!

A Simpler Life

MENDY MAYFIELD   Pascagoula

As I reflect on the events prior to and since Hurricane Katrina, I wonder what I would have done differently in choosing what to take with me, had I known the result would be that our home on the beach would be a bare slab when we returned. The extent of our loss was three houses, which are now slabs, and one other house that flooded, as well as the office and two cars. The initial bewilderment of the enormity of claims to process and adjusters to deal with was a huge adjustment and headache. But we are all safe, and that is the one thing that means most.

In retrospect, I would do as I did. We took our art collection, which makes us happy. It really doesn't fit the travel trailer we acquired after the storm, but it will be wonderful when we get into a house one day. We took family pictures, which are priceless. The rest of the stuff is just stuff. Good stuff, but just stuff. We live a much simpler life now in the trailer. We are happy. We haven't bought many clothes because there isn't a place to store them. We really haven't needed many and that is fine, too. We've picked up memories from our slab and shed a tear for the life we had which has been irrevocably changed. Still, we sit on our sea wall and gaze at the view we've loved for thirty years. Pascagoula will come back, as will the rest of the Gulf Coast. For now, the flavor is gone. Things have been put on hold until "normalcy" returns. I think it will be a long time before our beloved Gulf Coast is back. We'll rebuild, smaller and maybe better, as we reach into ourselves and find what truly makes us happy. I know that I miss my koi pond and my yard full of tropical plumeria, bird-of-paradise, and other tropicals which I tended and loved. These are the things that I want and need now! The rest is superfluous. The sunsets are still awesome, as is the sunrise. We can go on because we still have the good things that a storm named Katrina can't take from us.

ATTITUDE ADJUSTMENT

MELANIE REIMER MOORE   Pascagoula

In October, my friend Lib Roberts invited a group of us for a weekend at her family's house on Lake Martin. Lib had moved from Pascagoula to Atlanta in June and thus had escaped Katrina. But she was hurting for all of us and thought a getaway would be good therapy. She was right. To laugh in the face of adversity is to claim victory over it. And did we laugh!

One night we sat around describing our experiences and new way of life to Lib. We entertained her with excerpts from conversations which had become commonplace to us in our post-Katrina world. We found these little phrases hilarious, because prior to the storm none of us had ever uttered them. And now? We said them or responded to them about fifty times every day.

We poured a glass of wine, made our list, and laughed until we were hurting. Here is a sampling:

"Have you heard from FEMA?"
"Have you gotten your FEMA check yet?"
"Have you gotten your trailer yet?"
"Is your trailer hooked up yet?"
"Does your trailer have a pop-out?"

We soon found ourselves forming a Jeff Foxworthy–type list. Here is our collection:

You Might be a Katrina Victim If . . .

You start a lot of sentences with "I used to have . . ."

You might be a Katrina victim if you know what shud is. (You don't know what shud is? Shud is what you get when the storm surge causes all the toilets in your town to back up and overflow while at the same time the surge washes mud in though your front door. These two mix together to form "shud.")

You might be a Katrina victim if you know exactly what shud smells like. Or if you find creative ways to use this new word: "That insurance adjustor is full of shud." "Well, that's a shuddy deal."

You might be a Katrina victim if you have FEMA on speed dial, or if you look at your neighbor's load of Sheetrock with envy, or if you have been told multiple times by any and every agency, entity, or workman: "No, but you're on the list!"

You might be a Katrina victim if you have watched the following TV interview with two results:

Interviewee: "It's gawn."
Reporter: "What do you mean it's gone?"
Interviewee: "It's just all gawn!"

And you have (1) practiced saying "gawn," and (2) you know what "gawn" looks like.

You might be a Katrina victim if some of your best friends are homeless people, if in your mind the phrase "shock and awe" has absolutely nothing to do with Iraq, if your revised hurricane preparation list now includes a rubber dinghy, an axe, and a whistle, if you are addicted to the very cell phone you only tolerated before

8/29/05, if you are still wearing your nice earrings but are wearing other people's cast-off clothing and are thrilled to have it.

You might be a Katrina victim if you think back on the day someone advised you not to buy flood insurance because "if *your* house floods the whole town will be *gawn*," and you now wonder, "Yeah. So what's your point?"

You might be a Katrina victim if you swear you will never waste ice again.

You might be a Katrina victim if you stand in profound silence and cry as vehicles pass by that are labeled Georgia Power Co., Antioch Baptist Church of Chillicothe, Ohio, Indiana Brotherhood of Electrical Workers, New Jersey Power and Light, First Church Disaster Recovery of Chattanooga, Tennessee, or Fayetteville, North Carolina, or Greenville, South Carolina, or Palm Desert, California, and on and on . . . and you make a silent vow that you will go and help someone else when they have a disaster.

June 2006, Pearlington

Remains of the Bailey home after
cleaning out the totally flooded house.
John Golding, foreground.

June 2006, Bay St. Louis
First Presbyterian Church volunteers
eating after a long day of work

June 2006, Bay St. Louis
Helping to clean up: Steve Golding (left) and Meredith Spencer

June 2006, Bay St. Louis
The great spirit of survival. Ann and
Bobby Ladner.

June 2006, Bay St. Louis
Recalling horrors of Katrina. Ann Ladner
(right) and Jennifer McCarlie.

June 2006, Pearlington
Mud from tidal surge left in crystal
stemware, Lyn Bailey home

June 2006, Pearlington
Interior of historic First Missionary
Baptist Church ten months after the
storm

June 2006, Biloxi
Historic Biloxi Lighthouse in the distance
through the trees that were just growing
their leaves back

July 2006, Pass Christian
People still living in tents

August 2006
FEMA trailer park

August 2006, Gulfport
Tugboat/gift shop from Hurricane
Camille

THE MOTEL 8 ON CLEVELAND AVENUE

SUSIE W. MORAN   Ocean Springs

When Katrina was upgraded to a Category 5 the day before it was to make landfall, we packed up the grandchildren and headed for Calloway Gardens in Georgia. Many of our Ocean Springs friends were already there; the fellows stayed behind to keep an eye on things, and the wives and children evacuated. We watched the storm unfold on the silent TV through the night as the children slept. The news grew worse and worse, and we packed up again and headed to my daughter's home in Chapin, South Carolina, where we doubled the number of residents living there.

We stayed for five weeks, the six of us, and then it was time to return. It was a mess, for all that the cleanup was well begun. So many lost so much. For us, among the hardest to lose was our beloved family camp house on Back Bay, where we have played, shrimped, fished, sailed, and entertained the world with business and church meetings for years. It's so hard to ponder building it all back, and difficult even to ponder the future.

I was most fortunate in that my house was the only one of my family homes still standing. The minor damage it sustained was quickly repaired, and it soon became known as Motel 8 on Cleveland Avenue.

Some engineers who had been sleeping on the beach came to stay. Then groups from Jackson, New Orleans, North Carolina, South Carolina, Pennsylvania, Colorado, Tennessee . . . and more. We needed them so much and they responded with open hearts.

Right after the storm our worst needs were for gas and cash. No banks, no ATMs. Gas was at a premium, if even available. There was no food and nowhere to stay for many; folks simply left the coast. The prediction is that a third of the population will exit for at least a time.

I've been through Camille, Elena, Frederic, and, while all were bad, they seem to be getting worse. How many times can we rebuild?

PROVIDENCE AND PRIORITIES

BETTY OSWALD   Ocean Springs

Into every life some rain must fall . . . what better time to recall this phrase than on August 29, 2005, when Hurricane Katrina brought disaster to Mississippi, Louisiana, and Alabama residents. Most folks in those areas would say that the wind and water on that day were more than anyone should have in a lifetime. But through this devastating experience we have been given the opportunity to reflect on what is really important in our lives . . . what are our priorities?

In mid-August my husband and I boarded a cruise ship for a long-awaited trip to Scotland and Ireland. Before leaving home, we took the usual storm precautions, fastening the storm shutters, other essential arrangements. Comfortable with preparations, we left the country with light hearts and full of anticipation for our upcoming travels. We were utterly unaware of how little we humans can anticipate the future.

In the course of our voyage and excursions ashore, I became acquainted with a skilled art teacher from California, who shared her talent by giving classes aboard the ship. I eagerly took part in class to understand watercolors as taught by my newfound friend.

But as my art classes progressed, so did Hurricane Katrina. By Saturday evening, August 27, my husband and I realized that our hometown of Pascagoula was in grave danger. E-mail and CNN kept us informed, and when it appeared that Pascagoula was predicted to receive a storm surge of twenty feet or greater, it was evident that we and our neighbors along the beachfront were facing a catastrophe of major proportions.

The world now knows of the devastation to the Gulf Coast. The loss of our home was but one tiny part of it. As we were unable to fly home until the ship docked on September 3, we decided to complete our daily itinerary, knowing full well what we faced when we returned to Pascagoula.

At Waterford, Ireland, an excursion took us to Waterford Castle, situated in the middle of an island. It was a beautiful sunny day to visit this centuries-old landmark, and though our hearts were back on the Mississippi Gulf Coast, we proceeded to absorb the history of our surroundings, room by room. When I entered the library, my eyes were drawn to the massive fireplace, and I was stunned by the carved inscription on the mantelpiece, which read:

IF OUR EARTHLY HOUSE OF THIS TABERNACLE IS DISSOLVED, WE HAVE A BUILDING OF GOD—A HOUSE, NOT MADE WITH HANDS, ETERNAL IN THE HEAVENS!

Bob was in an adjacent room and I called him to come quickly. Upon reading the inscription, Bob hugged me with an understanding embrace, and I said, "Somebody up there is trying to tell us something. This sets our priorities straight." I took a pad and wrote down the inscription so I would not forget a word of it. I wanted to have bookmarks printed with this verse to share with neighbors and friends.

During the following days and weeks back home, as we talked to neighbors and friends, it was evident that each had a deep and personal understanding of the truth contained in the message. As I shared the bookmark copies we were struck by the recipients' nearly unanimous statement: *"Stuff doesn't matter."* This expression was always made with a spiritual significance. Each had recognized the need and value of having their priorities in perspective!

Several days after returning to Pascagoula, I was thrilled to receive an e-mail via my daughter's computer. It was from my art instructor on the ship, expressing her continuing concern for us and saying that she wanted to paint for us a watercolor of our choice. We recently moved into a new home in Ocean Springs, where Sonja's Irish landscape occupies a position of prominence above our fireplace mantel.

PAINFULLY FUNNY

OPAL SMITH   Pascagoula

Can *you* find humor in the destruction and devastation of a storm? Well, I will say this. We are all really peeved at Katrina. She slipped into our town the other day, or perhaps I should say she *roared* in, bringing giant tides and winds.

As we stood in the aftermath of the storm in our backyard, which was strewn with brick, windows, doors, bathtubs, and rags-that-were-formerly-drapes, my husband said, "You know, I need a ladder." He turned to go to his workshop and suddenly remembered that he no longer had a ladder. Gone was the workshop, his ladder, his tools, his fishing gear, his golf clubs, and the trash cans, which we could have really used right then.

One of our neighbors walked up, and as he approached he reached down and picked up a pair of pliers from the muck. They were already rusted from the salt water. He handed them to my husband and said "Here, Gary, fix your house." We all laughed, and it was good to laugh.

We found two lawn chairs among the debris, and we sat down under a giant oak, battered but still standing, in our backyard. As we sat there still trying to comprehend all that we were experiencing, Gary and I recognized an enormous oak tree that had washed up from the front yard. It was now lying in our neighbor's yard, its huge ball of roots extended in our direction. There were all sorts of beautiful colors entwined in the roots. I looked at Gary and said, "I do believe I have spied my underwear." We laughed as tears streamed down our faces.

Things We Have Learned

We can all ride in one car.
A car can be a grocery store and a bed if need be.
One towel will dry everyone in the family.
Water is the best drink in town and nothing tastes better.
A bag of ice is better than a sack of gold.
Two outfits are all you need.
Your neighbor is a part of the family.
Ole Miss and Mississippi State folks can embrace and say I love you.
Four in a bed is not an orgy.
Being cool is a bit of heaven.
Everyone in the family gets along.
No one is thinking diet.
Mildew grows even faster than weeds.
Gloves and boots are necessary fashion accessories.
An ice chest makes an okay suitcase.
Everyone in the neighborhood has the same house.
Any brand of coffee will do.

A SALVADOR DALI LANDSCAPE

RUTH THOMPSON   Bay St. Louis

Henry, my grandson, wanted to play with the water hose. It was very hot, but there was a slight breeze from the feeder bands of Hurricane Katrina. We found a hose under the oak tree and proceeded to get soaking wet. Around noon my husband came out to the tree and said, "Sam said you have to leave." "Sam? Sam Cuevas?" I asked. "Yes," he said. Well, Sam had been dead for almost two years, and I felt like the blood had run out of me.

We went inside to pack, and fifteen minutes later we left for points east and north. Six hours later, having traveled only eighty miles, we found a room in Mobile. It was the first time I had ever evacuated for a storm.

When Katrina hit the Gulf Coast and destroyed my home, business, studio, gallery, and the only way I had of making a living, the last thing on my mind was "art." However, in less than two months (which now seems like two seconds) I realized that I had lost my creative outlet. When art supplies showed up in Bay St. Louis, my heart just sang!

After walking around inside of a Salvadore Dali painting for months on end, I found that the opportunity to release the demons in my spirit was akin to having a waterfall wash all of the ugliness from my soul.

BIGGER THAN KATRINA

STACEY M. WAITES Vicksburg

So strange the way things work out. How the threads of events can wrap and twist without one ever feeling their tug and pull. Making an offhand promise for a couple of days of Katrina volunteer work caught me, kept me, and changed me forever.

When my pastor tapped me, as a social worker and therapist, to give a couple of days of Katrina relief work, I said, "Sure—no problem." The First Presbyterian Church of Vicksburg, Mississippi, was already in the full swing of volunteerism. Supplies were rolling in and eighteen-wheelers were being loaded. Everyone in the church had seemed to find something to do. I really didn't have the time but it was easier to say OK. I thought a few days away would do me some good. I mean, how bad could it be? I made a quick call to my sister, Sherri Buchanan, my lifelong partner in every adventure, and off we went.

I had this fantasy of how the hurricane aftermath would be and what I would be doing. Surely this would be easier than loading an eighteen-wheeler in the church parking lot. I thought that the usual disaster social work was all that lay ahead, such as crisis intervention, some displaced persons, dealing with minor stress, trauma, and grief support. You know, the same stuff—just a different location. I was sent to the

First Presbyterian Church of Bay St. Louis to assist an overwhelmed pastor in reclaiming his church and congregation. The closer I got to my destination the more my confidence began to slip away. The total devastation was more than I could absorb.

I found the church to be strangely intact, like an island in a sea of indescribable destruction. The sanctuary of the church was without damage. No mud and no water, as if spared by the hand of God. The goals in the first days were simple. Support the pastor, clean up, and keep my promise to have a Sunday service. That was tough but doable and it got done.

One need led to another and another and another until I and so many of the other volunteers were caught up in the pace. Each day and each hour Katrina sent us a new person, and new problems were coming in faster than we could respond.

And then Pearlington, Mississippi, slapped me full in the face. Asked to locate and assist residents and volunteers in Pearlington, I thought I had seen it all until I arrived and was exposed to an entirely new level of destruction. In Bay St. Louis there were walls and roofs in many places. The people had something to which to anchor and most had some place to sleep and something to eat. With few exceptions, Pearlington was washed away by a thirty-foot storm surge. The people were living in mud with nothing except what they could scavenge from under and around the debris. There was a state of stunned shock on most faces. The sense of community had been washed away. There were few identifiable possessions, property, or personal documents left for anyone. No one was better off than another. In that void of incapacity, there was no real ability to help one another. One resident recalled how he saw an old woman pulling a boat through the receding waters. As she passed without a word exchanged, he saw her dead husband lying in the boat.

The shock of the people of Pearlington almost seemed contagious. The ability to focus and plan began to slip away as we picked our way through debris. With car windows down, we began to pass small groups of survivors. Their needs were so overwhelming and immediate that we were shocked back into our helping roles.

Once again I was handling the storm. I was prepared for Katrina, but . . . I wasn't prepared for Kaitlyn. Standing before me was a three-foot, thirty-pound, three-year-old in the middle of the street blocking the road better than any pile of debris. Dirty clothes, dirty face, and homeless; she had the courage and clarity so absent in the adults around her. Katrina had taken her white boots, her house, and her toys, but she had refused to surrender her smile and beauty to the storm.

"Do you have a tent? I need a tent!" I melted. Having no clue where to get this child a tent, I promised her she would have one, and the next day she did.

Kaitlyn became my point of contact for the town of Pearlington. She became the voice of the community, because if Kaitlyn needed it so did everyone else. She was afraid of the dark and it was very dark at night. She got the first one of more than four hundred generators. Now she had light in the night. Unwilling to tolerate the loss of her toilet, Kaitlyn once more insisted someone do something about it. Kaitlyn got the first toilet, and the rest of Pearlington obtained portable toilets shortly thereafter. Thanks again, Kaitlyn!

The pattern continued as it had begun. Each day I would make a point to pass by Kaitlyn's family tent to drop off some treat or necessity. What I was really doing was getting my Kaitlyn "fix" for the day. It wasn't only my heart she captured. I saw very big men reduced to putty in her hands. All work stopped at the relief center when a little pink bicycle appeared that was just her size. It was repaired, painted, and decorated with just the right size basket. Not one relief worker missed her first ride through the distribution center parking lot. That single bicycle became the first Christmas gift for many of Pearlington's children. Kaitlyn insisted on recovering from this hurricane. She saw no other possibility. She carried us all with her.

It became time for me to leave Pearlington as the initial crisis gave way to the slow rebuilding process. Leaving was both a relief and a heartbreak. Like combat veterans who shared a foxhole, none of us will ever be the same. We call, we visit, we take short trips back to the battlefield to see how things have changed. Our memories bring us laughter and tears as we make promises to "get together again some day soon." I know that all of the people and places will fade from memory over time, with the exception of that little girl, Kaitlyn. Her spirit is bigger and stronger than Katrina ever was.

GERMAINE'S PHRASES

GERMAINE WELDON   Ocean Springs

Sometimes the sadness is overwhelming. Hearts can be broken not just by lovers but also by the loss of a way of life. Is living too close to the water somewhat like living in an abusive relationship? Did I set myself up for heartbreak by choosing the wrong place to live, like a woman chooses the wrong man? Was I caressed by the warm sun and the soft breeze and foolishly ignored my instincts that one day, any day, it could all be washed away?

Are we such hopeless romantics that we cannot face the reality that the force that tore our homes and families away from us could strike again? Does the rest of the nation look at us as we look at the battered woman who believes her husband will never hit her again? Does the wind whisper sweet promises of a better life?

I lived in an artist's paradise. In the early evenings, neighbors gathered by the beach to watch the sun set. Seagulls perched on old piers always sounded as if they were laughing at us. Perhaps they were.

My true loss is not the loss of my possessions. My true loss is that the lifestyle I cherished has washed away.

A friend asked me if I had cried. I had forgotten to. I had to be strong for my son, my family. There wasn't time to cry. I will cry next year.

I told my son we had lost everything. I knew all day but I waited till the evening to tell him. I agonized on how to say it. There is no good way to tell a child that everything is gone. My heart still aches.

My sister went to Pass Christian. This is the town she grew up in. This is the town where her children played in the sun. There was no sound. There were no cars, no people, no birds. Only a whistling wind.

Sometimes I just want to go home. I want to go into my bedroom, close the door, and feel the coolness of the sheets. There is no door. There is no bedroom. I have no home.

I drove to Bay St. Louis to see my son's school. From the moment I left the interstate, I saw nothing but devastation. The closer I drove to the beach, the worse it looked. I cannot stay here. People are living in tents. There is no beach. There is no road. Only a deep, bottomless sadness.

My friend cries every day. She wakes up, goes downstairs, and sees all the work she must do. She doesn't know where to begin, so she cries. Her home flooded twice. Everything downstairs is ruined; everything upstairs is fine. She is so weary, so very tired of this schizophrenic life.

Sightseers walk on my property. They gawk at the destruction. They don't know that this is a grave, this is sacred ground. This was my home. I feel violated. Please go away.

My friend can't get close to God. She is so angry. She goes to her prayer group and prays. She feels disconnected.

We who love this place, this coast, these waters, are having to evaluate our lives. It might be easier to walk away and leave, start another life, somewhere safer. Staying here is hard. We remember our pain, our loss, each day.

After the storm, signs in bold letters immediately rose from the rubble: WE WILL ENDURE, WE WILL NOT BE BROKEN, WE WILL REBUILD. Newspaper editorials espoused our strength, our optimism, and our new, bigger, and better plans. How could they boast about our future when we were still mourning our past?

An uneasy feeling filled my days immediately after the storm. I did not know who survived. I did not know whose homes were destroyed. Phone lines were down. Cell phones worked only sporadically. Days went by before I heard from friends scattered across the country. The panic slowly went away with each contact, but the uneasiness remained. Too many lost everything. Too many were hurt. Too many died.

I walk down to the river every day now. I have to live in a town four hours away from the destruction, yet I am still drawn to the water. The water gives me solace, it gives me hope. How can one body of water hold so much promise yet another body of water cause so much pain?

I am standing in line at a checkout counter. The woman in front of me is joking about the destruction. She said it was God's way of punishing us for all our sinning. What sin did I commit? Was living too close to the water my sin?

My father was a sea captain. My father's father was a sea captain. We have always lived near the water. It is in our destiny. We don't know how to live anyplace else.

One day, my son said he could not breathe when he was away from the water. I knew it was time to go back.

My husband had stopped at the only jewelry store in Monticello, Mississippi, on his way to visit me for the first time after the storm. He bought me a pearl necklace, and when the jeweler learned of our loss, he scribbled our name on a scrap of paper and tucked it in his pocket. He said he would add us to his prayer list. It's comforting to know we are on a prayer list, and we don't even know anyone in that town.

The debris is piled eighteen feet high. My home is somewhere in that pile. A Corps of Engineers worker is directing how it will be removed. He looks troubled. He tells me he doesn't know what to say. He has never seen anything like this before.

I found my sewing box in front of a church a half block from my home. All of the little compartments are still neatly intact. I can't make sense of this.

All these volunteers have driven long distances; they are sleeping in tents, giving their time, their gifts to us. They know this storm did more than wash away our homes. Armed with tool belts, they know they are not just repairing our homes, they are here to repair our souls.

The depth of the devastation has forced us to find the beauty in each of us.

SARA'S STORY

MARTI ANDERSON COCKRELL   Arlington, Texas

Our mother's home was swept away by Katrina. The house was built by our dad, her late husband of fifty-two years, in the early forties. It was rammed earth, inspired by a government pamphlet that he'd seen once, which described a house that had turned to stone, he used to tell us. He had built it in the hopes that it would turn to stone, too, and last through anything. After Katrina, there was nothing left of the house but the bricks of the front porch and the cement foundation.

Our dad, J. McConnell Anderson, was one of the Shearwater Pottery Andersons of Ocean Springs. And now all his precious artwork that she'd carefully saved over the years is gone. All the linoleum blocks, prints, wood carvings, pottery that he'd so beautifully decorated, his handmade cypress furniture. All just gone. It was, as everyone described over and over, "like a war zone." Devastated, but, strangely, somehow sacred at the same time, purified. "Matter became Spirit," to quote our cousin Mary.

Mama was in the hospital overnight for a shelter during Katrina. She was soon to be ninety-five years old, has congestive heart failure and needs oxygen to sleep well, so they let her in to the shelter, thank goodness. She was terrified of being in the house during a hurricane, after Camille. They had stayed for that one.

After Katrina passed, there was no phone communication for several very long days. Then, one day, my sister, Adele, got through long enough to shout, "Everything's gone!" That was all, the phone disconnected, and she was gone again. We weren't sure at all what that meant.

Finally, communications improved enough to get a better image of the situation. We immediately got into high gear and prepared to go and help out. We had to bring in all the gasoline we would need while there and enough to get out again, they told us. "Water and food as well. Everything you can think of that Mama might need. Clothes, nightgowns, she only has one. Her purse needs replacing, it was in the house. Bring food that doesn't need refrigeration, there's no electricity. Bring all the low- or no-salt stuff you can think of, she doesn't have any of that right now."

So, we went to get Mama and bring her home with us to Texas. She'd not lived anywhere except that house for over sixty years. For the last seven of those years, since our dad died, she'd lived virtually alone. My sister was with her, or a sitter. Quiet, surrounded by beauty and nature sounds. Occasionally a noisy boat launch across the harbor. She usually went to bed around 7, maybe 8 at the latest. She was the center of that universe.

She came to live with us in Arlington. It's never quiet here, with a houseful of kids. She's confused a good bit of the time. Sometimes very, very sad about her losses. Sometimes she just misses Papa and cries for him to help her. But, sometimes, incredibly, she is alert, herself, and says she knows she's better off here. She realizes there's no place for her there, and she was lonely anyway, most of the time. She's glad, at those times, to be here in Texas, but wonders wistfully if she'll ever see Ocean Springs again, where she grew up, worked at Shearwater for years, married and raised her two girls. She says she wants to be buried there. Mama loves to sit and watch the birds, and says we have a beautiful yard. There's one amazingly uplifting, beautiful new addition to this otherwise mostly sad story. Mama's very first great-grandchild, Bella, was born a couple weeks before Christmas, and is always an absolutely guaranteed, unfailing antidepressant, no matter what. So far, we are all managing.

We are doing everything we can to make Mama feel comfortable and safe. Sometimes she understands that and appreciates it very much. What an inconceivable experience for a ninety-five-year-old woman! We all remind ourselves often how many people were affected by that storm, and how many people are so much worse off than we are. It's mind-boggling, and we just pray that, somehow, good eventually comes out of it all.

April yet again

MARIA BAISIER   New Orleans

Spring has come again to the Gulf Coast, and T. S. Eliot was correct in saying that April is the cruelest month. April is resurrection. April is festival. It is frivolity and innocence. The month reminds us that everything can be new again. The cruelty lies in being unsure of all those things.

On August 29, 2005, an area of America the size of England was laid waste. The lives of 1.3 million Americans were changed forever by the wrath of Hurricane Katrina, and three weeks later, much of what Katrina did not take was destroyed by Hurricane Rita. There are 238,000 houses lying in ruin in New Orleans, and whole towns are gone from the Mississippi shore line. It is hard to be lighthearted this April. An autumn and a winter have come and gone, and we are becoming a distant memory in the minds of most Americans. It is said that the communal memory is thirty days. We are way beyond that.

A friend's daughter at college in Maryland was told by people on campus that Katrina is old news and "those people down there need to get on with it." Those people up there are right. But how exactly do we get on with it when "it" is gone? Where is Pass Christian? Where is

Waveland? Where are the dynamic businesses and stately mansions of Biloxi? Biloxi. Born before America, in 1699.

In New Orleans, also older than America, Canal Boulevard, a broad and beautiful thoroughfare running like a ribbon through a gorgeous neighborhood called Lakeview, has been manicured by the city, and its surviving trees are in bloom. It is beautiful to see. But the houses standing on both sides of the boulevard are empty. Some have had the sense to cave in; many list to one side like prisoners of war on some death march. Others were exploded by tornadoes. They are all dying under the weight of the water that cut off their oxygen for nearly a month. But April brings hope, and the houses' owners are trying to come home and rebuild their charming and vital community. But it will not be accomplished anytime soon. The owners are met with daily doses of frustration over insurance payments, federal buyouts, shortages of contractors, and undelivered FEMA trailers that would provide them a place to live while they rebuild. The frustration has deteriorated from shouts of anger to quiet resignation and determination.

April finds us watering this earth we love with our tears. In the Christian faith, April brings the betrayal of Jesus, his death, and his resurrection on Easter. We people of the Gulf Coast have followed a very similar path. We have felt deserted and betrayed. We have seen the deaths of some family members from the stress of this nightmare, the deaths of some friends, cities, towns, cultures, and lifestyles. We have watched as the sorrowing mother watched, knowing there is nothing we can do to stem the suffering of so many. And we have felt entombed. Closed away while the rest of the world moved on. Yet we are hopeful.

Each day brings some tiny progress to our region. It may be a reopened business, a reoccupied home, a replanted rice field, a rediscovered heirloom. Then our tears turn into laughter. And as we laugh, we remember the history of our region. We have risen before. From the brutality of war and the inhumanity of slavery, we have risen. From yellow fever plagues and the raging floods of the Mississippi River, we have risen. From the horrors of hurricanes Audrey, Betsy, and Camille, we have risen. And we shall rise yet again. Each month will be April as we re-create ourselves and our portion of America. The tears caught in our throats will become shouts of joy as we rush along the way to tell everyone of the resurrection and the new day that is surely dawning.

LANDSCAPES AND MINDSCAPES

ANN GUICE   Biloxi

Everyone has his or her own personal policies and procedures for life's audit. Compliance personnel have rules and regulations that check, cross-check, and use dual controls for each event. I wonder if the mentally ordered have handled chaos this massive and displacement with greater ease. Or do the creative minds, which seek no order but see designs where others don't, fare better? The lack of color is disturbing to many, especially the drought brown. Yet some artists choose to express themselves with little color as a method to dramatize the scene. Do our mindscapes dictate our landscapes, or does nature ordain our emotions?

While taking a noon stroll to the harbor, I felt my path was clearer and less obstructed. I only had to walk around or over smaller piles of trash. I was pretty excited when the shrimp boat was removed from the street and the bricks were piled where an office had been. I enjoyed the reading garden on the Biloxi Town Green and absorbed the sun, breeze, and smells of the salty gulf. But I had to keep the tunnel vision in cruise control to avoid the destruction on either side of the block. I'm proud I helped rake and clear the trash so others could also find this small oasis of relaxation. We need to have a sanctuary to rest our spirit and our bodies. The extended effort in surviving a work week is daunting. Even people who had no damage tell me they are exhausted dealing with the landscape, the change in routines, the new commutes and detours. If you are fortunate enough to have something to repair, the repairman never keeps the appointment but promises another day and time and fails to show again.

Have we become so accustomed to the awful that progress is measured only in terms of gross tons of trash removed? Will I live long enough to complain that the road wasn't edged?

Will we ever get to the point in reconstruction where the new obscures the rubble? My out-of-state vendors call and ask if I have finished rebuilding my home. I've spent ten months clearing my small lot, and it is still not free of fallen trees, concrete chunks, and trash wrapped around tree limbs. I rejoice in the progress yet scream in frustration at my lack of control and loss of patience. I can't get my own yard cleaned; how can we expect to clean the Mississippi coast? I believe in mind over matter and get up each day and believe progress can be seen. I choose to be happy. But is this new survival mechanism so strong I will forget life's artistic and cultural enrichment? Will I dance the dance but not hear the music?

My mindscape is pretty dependable. I've survived crisis and trauma, heartbreaks and bone breaks. But is survivability determined from within or without? I considered myself a seasoned survivor, but nothing prepared me for the emotional destruction of my home and all my possessions. Will we need the landscape to improve dramatically before our mindscape can accept the change? I gravitate to green space and flower pots, bright colors and order. I still drive through neighborhoods with cranes, bulldozers, front-end loaders, and lopsided dump trucks littering their wake. For years I looked forward to seeing a tiny garden in front of a home on my way to work. I was extremely saddened to pass and see the house totally destroyed last August. The garden was under rubble, and months passed before I even saw the elderly lady gardener. But each day this tiny lady worked in her garden after the lot was cleared and her trailer connected to pipes and wires. Each day she watered and tended her small oasis. Summer heat arrived and the blooms are glorious. One morning I pulled over and thanked her for her efforts in the garden. I thanked her for making my daily commute more pleasant and inspired. I thanked her for her courage and the colors of her spirit. Now each day I wave to my new friend. I don't know her name and know she does not remember mine. We would have never spoken a year ago—it was just a modest yard in an older neighborhood and I was always in a hurry. Now I get excited about the detour to home, and instead of shrimp boats on the sound I see zinnias, marigolds, and salvia. I wonder if she realizes how much her efforts mean. One landscaped garden at a time will take an eternity. Will our mindscape survive?

JOEY HAMMOCK HALINSKI   Vicksburg

In 1998, we moved our family from Arkansas to Vicksburg, Mississippi. It was hard leaving family and friends, but from the beginning, we loved Vicksburg. It was a major transition for our three sons, Daniel, Alex, and Peter Michael, but they adjusted well to a new school and new friends.

Daniel, our oldest, is a fine student and an even better athlete. He loved any type of sports and worked very hard at improving his skills. He started playing football and was the quarterback in the seventh grade for St. Aloysius's junior high team; he would keep this position all the way into his senior year, 2005.

Though modest and not one to relish being the center of attention, he nevertheless became an inspiring leader for the team. His younger brother Alex was the star linebacker, and together they played hard and, if possible, became even closer. He put in long, hard hours trying to be the best he could be for this 1-A high school and his team, the Flashes. If he did well, the fans loved him; if he messed up, the fans hated him. It was hard for us as parents to watch our son deal with this type of pressure, but he handled it with his usual grace.

Then came Hurricane Katrina and all the havoc that was unleashed as she ravaged Mississippi. In Vicksburg, we had the least of it. We had trees down, no electricity, and great inconvenience, but we were basically whole. The following days would bring much TV watching as we tried to figure out the extent of the devastation. We realized that the people from New Orleans and the Gulf Coast who evacuated to Vicksburg wouldn't be returning home any time soon, as it became apparent they might not have anything left to return to! The people of Vicksburg rallied. We helped them with temporary homes, groceries, clothes, medicine, school supplies, etc.

St. Aloysius High School received over fifty new students. They were from every walk of life—some from New Orleans and some from the Gulf Coast. It was overwhelming for the students and their families. The first few days they took it all in stride as an adventure, but then the reality set in. These families were in it for the long haul. Their depression became apparent. School was a great normalizer for these families. St. Aloysius, the students, faculty, teachers, and parents did all they could and more to help our new friends.

Three of these new students were from a 5-A all boys' Catholic school. Two were seniors. What a way to begin their senior year! Since their schools were badly damaged, they signed up for football at St. Al. The Mississippi Sports Association gave a special dispensation to the evacuees in Mississippi so the kids could play. We were one of the few schools who actually let the kids play; other teams just let them dress out and ride the bench.

The St. Al's team and coaches were ecstatic. The entire school made sure they were welcomed in every way—that they had uniforms, that their photos were in the football program, and that they were included in pep rallies. One of these boys was a quarterback. Without our knowing, our son told the coaches he would share the position of quarterback. At first, we were unsure about his decision. He had worked many years to get to this point in his football career. The *New York Daily News* flew in a reporter to interview our son, his teammates, and the coaches. The person was brutal, trying to get them to say something negative about these kids coming in and taking their positions. The team took the high road, and their comments were positive and encouraging. After all, these new teammates had lost their school, homes, fans, and everything that comes with Friday night football.

Some Friday nights we won, but there were also many losses. If Daniel was doing well, it was a friendly crowd; if he made errors, they would yell the other kid's name. The fans would whisper, "Why don't they let the other kid play, he's from a 5-A school and much better." It was tough, but through it all my son had the conviction to share, to give up his senior year, to take the brunt of the losses. The uglier the crowd was, the closer the teammates became. They were great friends. They hung out together after the games, and the parents also forged lasting friendships.

At the end of the season and the beginning of the new year we were given the news that the evacuee seniors had to return to their broken school. If not, they couldn't graduate with a degree from the school they had attended their entire high school career. We were crushed, and they were, too. The kids left, and it was a very sad time. But they could return! They came to Vicksburg for the prom and brought their dates; they came on weekends to see their friends, and they are returning for the senior retreat with permission from their school. They may have only been here a few months, but what an impact they left on our/their school!

And what an impact our son left on us. In all this time not only did he take the high road, but he was right. These kids, our kids, their courage, our goodness, it was a great life lesson! My son, I am proud to say, became a man without our meddling!

In March 2006, we took our children and family members to the Gulf Coast to see the damage. The television and newspaper coverage were good, but in order to understand the severity and the enormity of Hurricane Katrina you had to see the damage firsthand. My sons were visibly moved, as are we all. As the days go on, the small silver linings are starting to show through, and the rebuilding begins.

Postscript: In May 2006, the St. Aloysius Athletic Awards were held. All the seniors were honored, and the three seniors from New Orleans were asked to come back and be part of the awards ceremony. John Buckman won the award for Most Versatile; Chris Baer won the award for Best Defensive Back; Noah Slater won the award for Most Valuable Player for Defense. Noah was also chosen to play in the Mississippi All-Stars game and will play college football. And our son, Daniel Halinski, won the most prestigious football award given to a St. Al football player: the Virgadamo Award. This award is given to a senior for leadership, athletics, academics, and HEART!

CONNECTIONS

DELL DICKINS SCOPER Laurel

In his provocative book *Connect*, on the emotional well-being of our society, Dr. Edward Hallowell asserts that what sustains us as human beings is a sense of connectedness, the feeling that we are a part of things that matter, something larger than ourselves that gives life meaning and direction. These connections, Dr. Hallowell concludes, are accomplished through human moments.

The aftermath of Katrina provided us "human moments" in abundance, in our neighborhoods, churches, workplaces—all over our great state. And Mississippians, inspired by Governor Haley Barbour's now-familiar statement, "Well, folks, it looks like we've got to hitch up our britches and get going," did just that.

Mississippians have always known that the stuff we were made of is real. And we who have been sorely tested, in the days and months since Katrina came into our lives, now know that those thousands with caring hands and hearts who came from all over our nation to help us rebuild our lives are likewise very real. Our fellow Americans came through. The "stuff we're made of" was proven in the aftermath of 9/11 and, now, 8/29.

A Different Perspective

SARAH H. LISANBY, M.D. New York City

What we didn't lose, a partial listing:

One hurricane-burnished silver teapot
One saucer from our parents' wedding china pattern
One ceramic sculpture by a Mississippi woman artist borne
        to safety by the twenty-five-foot storm surge
Our mother's Patron of the Arts award
One baby photo and one wedding portrait of each sister
One portrait of our father in dress uniform
One angel figurine buried in the breached century-old foundation
One treasured childhood dollhouse

Walking to school on my own for the first time
Fishing with my father on a disappeared pier
Our childhood

Dear friends entertained and hospitality shared
Our mother's seventieth birthday celebration
Family gatherings at Christmas

Everything we gave to others

Prayers offered and answered

Our hope
Our faith
Our charity
Our parents
Our love
Our future

In short: everything important.

CLEARING

GERMAINE WELDON Ocean Springs

The Corps of Engineers came to my property yesterday to clear my debris field. Big strong men with soft hearts, a dump truck, and a forty-thousand-pound track hoe. The machinery was like some prehistoric monster, ripping concrete columns from the earth and tossing them on a pile of rubble. Every once in a while, the operator would gently pick up a battered treasure—a silver platter, a chair—and carefully place it away from the pile for me to take home. One engineer stood near me, his presence comforting. His broad sunburned face showed sadness. He knew this story. This had happened to him in another time, another place, another storm, but the pain was the same. I felt his kindness, his warmth, and was grateful for that. I did not want to leave his side. Together we stood, understanding that this storm did more than wash away some homes. The damage was far worse. A forty-thousand-pound track hoe could clear my lot, but it could not remove the emotional debris left behind.

CLOSURE, WYTHEFLAIR

GLADYS KEMP LISANBY   Pascagoula

After we had viewed the unsteady remains for more than seven months, the day finally arrived in March 2006 for our home on Beach Boulevard in Pascagoula to be torn down and hauled away by the U.S. Army Corps of Engineers.

This amazing home, named Wytheflair by my family, had survived many storms since its construction in 1898, and could have related many stories of our family gatherings, holidays, a military wedding, teas, a seventieth birthday party (mine), and, over the past ten years, many luncheon meetings and parties for the Mississippi State Committee of the National Museum of Women in the Arts.

As the morning began, the upstairs still stood proudly, for all that the first floor was off its foundation and all but destroyed by the effects of Hurricane Katrina.

Gathered around the scene was a collection of friends, curious strangers, and dozens of workers in hard hats with their cranes and trucks at the ready, all focused on the job at hand. I will always remember and be thankful for the respect and empathy displayed by all of those workers to me and to my husband, Jim.

Work began when the area was secured for safety purposes with bright yellow tape and sprinkled by a water hose to hold down the dust.

With one final request for our permission, the skilled operator positioned his large yellow crane in front of the house and attacked the upper story. After repeated blows, the first chimney finally crumbled, but the roof did not give up so easily. As work progressed, it was painful to see the blue wall of a favorite bedroom suddenly exposed, yet defiant with curtains still in place as though it did not want to be destroyed.

Once the task was complete, the crane operator drove to the top of the very tall debris pile and came back down with an antique bathtub with claw feet still in perfect condition. What a treasure and what a caring gesture from the crew. Two days and some fifty truckloads later, the site was finally cleared and only the magnificent view remains, which we now share from the steps of our FEMA trailer.

To me, closure is a word that has new meaning and I can move forward with all those happy memories of a full life shared with family and friends in Wytheflair on the beautiful Mississippi Gulf Coast.

HURRICANE KATRINA REFLECTIONS

ANN LISANBY BIANCHI   Huntsville, Alabama

Three days after the devastating news about our family's home in Pascagoula, my husband and I headed to the coast to assist my parents. The seven-hour car ride from Huntsville, Alabama, seemed endless. Along Interstate 65 we passed a long convoy of military vehicles and many telephone repair trucks. We were all a part of the recovery effort. My mind was filled with flashing images of what the house might look like and of the possible damage to the town of Pascagoula.

We spent the next few days busily crawling around in the dirt where the living room and dining room used to be. A dirt floor was all that Katrina had left, so our efforts were focused on salvaging anything that we could dig up. We were able to climb over piles of wood and other debris to rescue some things in the kitchen. It was amazing to see a refrigerator turned on its side and a double oven ripped out of the cabinetry in the same room where a plate still rested on a stand above the kitchen cabinets.

Hour by hour, it became clearer that the loss was significant. Each item recovered was a reminder of a lifestyle that once was enjoyed with friends and family but that now was changed forever.

On a normal day, going to Wal-Mart would be just an ordinary shopping trip. But in Pascagoula following the storm, a trip to Wal-Mart meant picking up supplies for cleaning salvaged goods and purchasing other items that would make very unsettled lives a little easier for the moment. More important, Wal-Mart was a place where one could see familiar faces and connect with neighbors who were impossible to get hold of by phone or e-mail. My mother ran into a friend who gave us an update on her situation. Her backyard was full of household items. Katrina had left nothing at all in our backyard, but since this friend lived a few blocks north of the gulf her backyard was filled. Unfortunately, none of these items had come from her own house.

Even though we know we should not focus on the material aspects of our loss, I feel that some of those things held a connection to our family's past. A sword may be just a sword, but it has meaning when it belonged to a great-grandfather who fought in the Civil War. The artwork by family members tells a story of what was important in the day when the paintings were done. Each is a reflection of that family member as a person and as an artist. Those things will be missed. A Virginia sofa that was once a gathering place for countless family reunions where stories were shared is gone, not even a piece of it recognizable in the huge pile of rubble. Place settings of china saved for the next generation are also gone. Countless objects that made a house a home are gone.

As I reflect on the experiences we had during a time of hardship, it is a comfort to know that what means the most to my family was not destroyed by Katrina. Our memories are tucked away for our mind's eye to see, and we can revisit them anytime we feel a need to connect. These memories will always be safe from rain, wind, and even storm surge.

CODA

MARY ANDERSON PICKARD   Ocean Springs

Hurricanes are integral to the Gulf Coast. Like beaches, marshes, sand-bars, heat, and humidity; like mosquitoes, live oaks and pines, the shining expanse of Biloxi Bay, and winter sunsets over tree-fringed is-lands; like crabs, shrimp, fish and oysters; hurricanes are intrinsic vital elements of this place.

My father, the artist Walter Anderson, was exhilarated by these great storms. "Why does man live?" he wrote. "[T]o judge between winter and summer which shall win the yearly war of the ellipse . . . to be a servant and a slave to all the elements." After spending Hurricane Betsy on Horn Island, he surveyed the flotsam, fallen trees, and eroded beaches, and summed up: "Louisiana's house-cleaning at the expense of Mississippi."

Hurricanes stimulate, shaking us and awakening us to a new aware-ness. The big winds do sweep our world and prune our vegetation. High tides flood our marshes and estuaries, flushing and cleansing, reform-ing the littoral; sometimes building new land, sometimes taking land away. Life where land meets sea is life on the edge—a chancy business. Perhaps the gambling boats are appropriate to the setting. People who choose to live here accept the risks, buy insurance and adjust their lifestyles. My uncle Peter built his pier in sections which could be dismantled and pulled by rope to higher ground as the tide rose.

Great hurricanes become markers in coastal lives—people remember Biloxi before the storm of 1947, the many changes wrought by Camille in 1969. Today we still grieve our losses and struggle to find balance. From now on, we will date our lives before and after Katrina.

In September of 1947, when I was nine years old, a crash and a shivery shower of rain and broken glass, followed by the sharp scent of wet cedar, sent me leaping from my bed into my mother's room. "Wake up! The hurricane is here!" I pressed my face against the windowpane, peering through the cracks in the hundred-year-old blinds at a grey world of flying rain and heavy swollen sea. Secure in my mother's presence, with the strength of the old house around me, I thrilled to the howling power of the wind, the crashing waves, the blown spatters of spray; crying only when the ancient live oaks fell, one by one, with the eroding bluff as the great house trembled.

In August 1969, I was thirty-six and had four small children. As I considered taking them to the shelter, wind gusts toppled a tall pine and broken electric wires flashed blue fire, and the first feeder bands, the horizontal sheets of rain, swept ashore ahead of Camille. Our escape was blocked and we spent a terrifying night cowering on a mattress under the dining room table. The walls of our small frame house flexed and creaked. The wind howled like banshees. Tornadoes roared and receded like freight trains. Five large trees cracked, whooshed, and crashed through our roof, opening us to the wind and rain. Only their weight kept the little house from flying away into the maelstrom. I prayed with clenched fists. When morning finally came, I was surprised to find my palms bloody, cut by my fingernails.

At Shearwater in 1979, too many trees fell to Frederic. During Elena in 1981, an unusual wind blew all the water from the bay, leaving an abstract pattern of black rectangles in the wet mud, which turned out to be abandoned crab traps. As curator to the family's Walter Anderson art collection, I suffered anxiety and upset stomach each time a storm entered the gulf. I breathed sighs of relief when the Walter Anderson Museum of Art was finished, and the painted room safely housed there; and when a "Camille-proof" vault was constructed on the Shearwater grounds. In September 1998 Hurricane Georges found me once again under a table, on a mattress this time in my son Mark's house, with my wiggly-giggly granddaughter Jeanne Elise beside me. Again I listened to the creaks and crashes, the spattering waves of rain, feeling the stressed movement of the walls under the pressure of rising winds.

Despite a certain shame—old-timers never leave the coast when storms come ashore—I evacuated for Ivan, and have done so for every serious storm since. On August 28 I drove to Hattiesburg to spend Katrina with my friend Nita. We lost power there at 8 a.m. on the 29th, as great pines fell on houses all around us. At 2 p.m. the creek overflowed, flooding the yard. At the door stoop I rescued a swimming shrew. Our battery-powered radio was erratic, our cell phones useless, and the agony of not knowing about the coast was worse that the storm itself. After several days spent in limbo at my son's hunting camp in Lexington, I drove down to Ocean Springs on Saturday, arriving at the tired end of the day to find my house, my home—life as I knew it—gone. It was a shock I have yet to assimilate even one year later.

The essays in this book have helped me. Reading them I felt a kinship of shared tragedy, of disbelief, horror, stunned sorrow, and angry helplessness. I too knew the disorienting effect described by Katherine Lochridge, when confronted by a world without familiar landmarks. Like Lyn Brown, I too had dreams which anticipated Katrina—in one my mother guided me over the ruins of the destroyed house called The Barn. Like these writers, I remember the Herculean effort of attempting to clean up, to find what we could in the terrible heat. Like Joan Armstrong, I felt the fascination of mountains of debris, the precarious balance of splintered wood, exposed nails, and torn sheet metal. Did we think that under the next board we'd find the meaning, the treasure worth saving, a secret to restore our ruined lives?

As I read I recognized anew the value of basic things: water, ice, a place to sleep; shade, food, and the kindnesses of friends and strangers. Like Joan, Kristin Byrd, and Joey Halinski, I found new reason to be proud of my sons, who proved themselves again and again. Both Mark and Chris gave me blessed shelter, and worked endlessly at the cleanup. For my son Jason the restoration of his beloved Shearwater Pottery became a personal calling. He has rebuilt the old workshops with touching care and fidelity, sleeping each night in a tent on the property. Early mornings he drank coffee by a campfire and wrote songs. His poignant lyrics evoke those early months. He sings of "your perfect world gone strange," and "a shred of fabric from a dress she looked so fine in, tangled in a shattered tree he learned to climb in." He titled his songs "What Remains," "Temporary," and—for a musical benefit in California—"Give A Little." My cousin's daughter, Beth Ashley, arrived from her Nashville job as a problem-solver for a large communications company, and threw herself into solving the problems of our extended family. She gently, but firmly, pushed and guided us in our zombie-like state through our first dealings with insurance companies, FEMA, and the Red Cross. I appreciate the jokes that alleviated the frustrations these essayists encountered when dealing with these entities. I encountered them, too.

Humor is a safety valve. We sometimes laugh to keep from crying. I laughed at the incongruous image of Opal Smith "finding" her underwear hanging in the upended roots of her overturned live oak, and at Lyn Bailey's underwear signaling and attracting the rescue helicopters that "found" Pearlington. I delighted in the brave spirit reflected in writings by Ann Guice, Marjie Gowdy, and Patt Odom. Sarah H. Lisanby's list of "what we didn't lose" prompted me to make a list of my own. Gladys Kemp Lisanby's beautiful farewell to her past shines with the real grace of acceptance.

Many writers, and especially the artists among them, speak of the colorless state of our Gulf Coast world—"like a sepia photograph"—leafless, scorched by salt, and coated in the grey-brown mud that smelled of decay. Signs of recovery seemed long in coming. We all rejoiced in the explosion of green shoots, evidence of the presence of life, which came in the months after the storm. "'Hope' is the thing with feathers," wrote Emily Dickinson. Like Germaine Weldon, I found the insistent cheerful words, broadcast on TV and plastered over newspapers, precipitous and intrusive on my mourning. But hope *is* intrusive and insistent. It "sings the tune without the words— / And never stops—at all—." Perhaps the spirit prompting the slogans and flags *does* fuel the recovery. Like Ann Arledge, I know my own soul began to heal when the birds came back again.

These writers hail the arrival of spring and the healing power of flowers and gardens. What of the terrible months without rain, when drought finished off many trees already damaged by the storm? And what of those damaged people, who survived the tempest but died suddenly or slowly in the months that followed? I know people who suffered no visible loss or damage, but who had to live in the midst of devastation, and are only now realizing how much they were affected. They suffer depression and anxieties which, as the summer ages and the anniversary of the storm nears, become more acute.

When I was a child I sat on my grandmother's screen porch, mesmerized by my favorite of her stories—L'Ile Derniere and the hurricane of 1856. Last Island, a summer resort for wealthy planters and New Orleanians, was swept away by that storm while its beautifully dressed visitors waltzed and waltzed around the hotel ballroom. In 1947 I danced in the great hall at Oldfields, as the wind roared. Rain and spray pelted the house. Trees fell as the high bluff melted away in the surge, and my childhood ended.

Today I stood before a foundation wall in the ruins of my pre-Katrina home at Shearwater, where my father's studio house stood before Camille. I reread the dedication we printed in the concrete:

> Be sustained by the love which set you close to the waves, open to the sun, the wind, the islands, and the great gulf beyond.

Did we tempt fate? Do all who rush to build where sea meets land do so with an audacity beyond optimism? Global warming is an actuality. I have watched the land in front of my Shearwater house disappearing as tides grow higher each year. I have felt the gulf water at Horn Island, warm as soup in August. Could this catastrophic storm be a catalyst for environmental awakening?

In her essay, Susie Moran asks tiredly, "How many times will we rebuild?" Germaine Weldon likens our insistence on coastal living to staying in an abusive relationship, but her young son says he can't breathe away from water. In the past I would have said the same, but Katrina has set me free. I will not rebuild on my property. Arkansas tempted me. I found a place there, and planned to go. Like Gerard Manley Hopkins's nun, I had had enough.

> And I have asked to be
> Where no storms come,
> Where the green swell is in the havens dumb,
> And out of the swing of the sea.

But I recognized in time that life is "on the edge" no matter where one lives. I found a house in Ocean Springs, a mile and a half from the beach, but near a bayou. I have a small woods, with cane and palmetto, and a tiny pond. Rabbits, turtles, opossums, raccoons, a king snake, and many birds share my world. In the words of a poem I wrote after Camille, "I have pulled my boat much higher up the beach, and tied it to a taller tree."